Good Housekeeping Institute
TRIED · TESTED · TRUSTED

Good Housekeeping
CHOCOLATE

100 INDULGENT DESSERTS, CAKES, COOKIES AND TREATS

COLLINS & BROWN

First published in Great Britain in 2002
by Collins & Brown Limited
64 Brewery Road
London N7 9NT

A member of **Chrysalis** Books plc

Published in association with
The National Magazine Company Limited.
Good Housekeeping is a trade mark of
The National Magazine Company Limited.

1 3 5 7 9 8 6 4 2

British Library Cataloguing-in-Publication Data:
A catalogue record for this book is available from the
British Library.

ISBN 1 85585 983 1

Project manager: Gillian Haslam
Project editor: Janet Illsley
Designer: Nigel Soper
Techniques photographer (pages 9-13): Craig Robertson
Food stylist (pages 9-13): Joanna Farrow

Reproduction by Bright Arts Pte Ltd, Singapore
Printed and bound by Canale & C Spa, Italy
This book was typeset using Futura and Joanna

NOTES

- Both metric and imperial measures are given for the recipes. Follow either set of measures, not a mixture of both, as they are not interchangeable.
- All spoon measures are level.
  1 tsp = 5ml spoon; 1 tbsp = 15ml spoon.
- Ovens must be preheated to the specified temperature.
- Large eggs should be used except where otherwise specified. Free-range eggs are recommended.
- The use of golden granulated, caster and icing sugar is recommended.
- Some of the desserts contain raw or lightly cooked eggs. The young, elderly, pregnant women and anyone with an immune-deficiency disease should avoid these, because of the possible risk of salmonella.

ONTENTS

FOREWORD   6

A GUIDE TO CHOCOLATE   8

CHOCOLATE TECHNIQUES   10

HOT PUDDINGS   14

COLD DESSERTS   36

EVERYDAY CAKES   74

SPECIAL OCCASION CAKES   102

SWEET TREATS   120

INDEX   142

FOREWORD

There are times when only chocolate will satisfy. My favourite variety for nibbling on is a particular brand of rich dark chocolate with an intriguing blend of spices. And you can be sure that whenever you serve a homemade chocolate pudding, it will always be met with sighs of delight.

My favourite recipe in this book is probably the simplest. It's for those impromptu moments when you've eaten your main course, yet you still feel the need something else to complete the meal. Turn to page 38 for our rich chocolate pots – you only need a couple of ingredients so you can make it whilst your guests are sitting at the table. Warm, melted chocolate is stirred into double cream, and mixed with mascarpone and a dash of cognac, then poured into mini glasses and topped with crème fraîche and a chocolate curl. Yummy!

It's no mistake that we've included several recipes for chocolate cakes, chocolate soufflés and so on, because we at Good Housekeeping strive for perfection. We triple-test every recipe to guarantee success – and know that subtle differences in the ingredients can create a lighter, squidgier or richer result. So there's plenty of choice here for you to discover your own favourite.

Have fun!

Felicity

FELICITY BARNUM-BOBB

COOKERY EDITOR

A GUIDE TO CHOCOLATE

There is an extensive range of chocolate products available today, from the intense, cocoa-rich chocolates produced in Belgium, Switzerland and France, to the sweeter, milkier confections manufactured in the UK. But whatever your preference, there's no doubt that when it comes to cooking, the dark, continental varieties produce the best results for most purposes.

Quality is partly determined by the percentage of cocoa solids. The lower the cocoa solids, the higher the proportion of cocoa butter and lesser ingredients, such as added vegetable fat, sugar and additives. A fine plain chocolate, produced by Valrhona, for instance, will consist of 60-70% cocoa solids, plus sugar and, perhaps, some natural vanilla flavouring. No powdered milk, no unspecified vegetable fats, nothing to detract from the true flavour of the cocoa bean.

But if a high percentage of cocoa solids is the most obvious indicator of quality, it's by no means the only determining factor. Equally important is the quality of the raw materials, in this case cocoa beans, and the way they are harvested and handled during the manufacturing process. Top producers are meticulous in their selection and treat the beans with care as they are roasted, shelled and ground to the paste that forms the basis for their chocolates. The choice of cocoa beans is yet another variable but, like fine wine and coffee, most quality chocolate is the result of a careful blending process, the precise details of which are often kept a closely guarded secret.

Choosing chocolate, then, is no simple matter. Cooking with chocolate raises more vexing questions. Which is the best sort to use? Is fine quality chocolate wasted on baking? Does the term 'chocolate flavour cake covering' imply an inferior product? In general, you will get what you pay for, but it helps to have an understanding of the different types of chocolate you can buy.

Couverture is the chocolate preferred by chefs and chocolatiers. Rich in cocoa solids, it also has a high percentage of cocoa butter (at least 34%), which gives a melt-in-the-mouth quality, a lustre and viscosity that transforms sauces and liquid coatings. However, it is expensive and only available from specialist suppliers.

Dark, bitter chocolate with its high proportion (70–85%) of cocoa solids is quite bitter because it contains little sugar. Most supermarkets stock their own-brand version (typically 72% cocoa solids), labelled 'continental' or 'dark, bitter chocolate', as well as proprietary brands. This type of chocolate melts to a glossy, smooth consistency and has a rich, intense flavour. It is perfect for sauces, ganache and most sweets, cakes and desserts, except creamy mousses that would set too firmly, and where a gentle flavour is called for.

Bitter sweet chocolate containing 60–70% cocoa solids is also ideal for most chocolate recipes. It melts to a thin, dark sauce, but has a smooth, creamy texture and a good balance of sweetness and bitterness. This chocolate is ideal for mousses and soufflés, as the bitterness is mellowed by the addition of eggs and butter, but the intense flavour still comes through.

Ordinary plain chocolate containing 30–55% cocoa solids has a less intense, sweeter taste. It is suitable for most cakes and biscuits.

Ordinary milk chocolate has a mild, sweet flavour and contains around 20% cocoa solids. Its gentle flavour makes it less suitable for cooking, though it can be melted carefully to make decorations. Fine quality milk chocolate, containing about 40% cocoa solids, is obtainable; this is suitable for creamy puddings, such as mousses and soufflés.

White chocolate contains no cocoa solids, but derives its taste from a high cocoa butter content. Superior quality white chocolate gives a rich, smooth flavour, but must be melted with care.

Chocolate flavour cake covering is produced from a blend of vegetable oil, cocoa, sugar and flavourings. It has a somewhat synthetic flavour.

STORING CHOCOLATE

Chocolate should be kept well wrapped, in a cool, dry place. If stored incorrectly, in warm or humid conditions, it is liable to develop an unattractive white 'bloom'.

MELTING CHOCOLATE

Chocolate can be melted over hot water, or in a microwave. Either way, you must avoid over-heating, or water coming into contact with the chocolate, causing it to develop a grainy texture, or 'seize' into a solid mass. Particular care must be taken with white chocolate. If you need to add water, milk or alcohol, then you must do so before you melt the chocolate. If you add these afterwards, you risk 'seizing'.

Break up the chocolate or chop it into small pieces and put in a heatproof bowl. Put over a pan of gently simmering water, making sure the bowl does not touch the water otherwise the chocolate will get too hot. Leave until melted; don't be tempted to stir the chocolate as it melts.

Once melted, stir the chocolate until smooth and remove the bowl from the pan. Standing the bowl in a warm place is usually sufficient to keep the chocolate melted.

To melt chocolate in a microwave break it into pieces, put it in a bowl and microwave on high, allowing about 2 minutes for 125g (4oz). It is safer to melt white and milk chocolate on a low setting, allowing 4–5 minutes for 125g (4oz). (These timings apply to a 650W oven.)

To melt chocolate with cream you can either melt the ingredients together, or heat the cream and pour it on to the chocolate to melt it (the traditional way of making a chocolate ganache).

Break up the chocolate and put it in a bowl. Bring the cream to the boil, then slowly pour it on to the chocolate and stir gently, until the chocolate has melted and the mixture is smooth.

CHOCOLATE TECHNIQUES

TRADITIONAL CHOCOLATE CURLS
Chocolate curls, or 'chocolate caraque', make an effective decoration for cakes and cold desserts. Use plain, dark chocolate containing at least 70% cocoa solids, or a good quality white or milk chocolate.

Melt the chocolate and spread it in a thin, even layer on a marble slab, or clean, smooth work surface. Leave until the chocolate is just set, but not until it is solid.

When the chocolate has just set, push a large knife across it at an angle of about 20° to shave off curls. (Or you can use a clean decorator's wallpaper stripper instead of a knife.)

Carefully transfer the curls to a tray lined with greaseproof paper. If the chocolate breaks, rather than forms curls, it has set too firmly and will need to be melted again. Store the curls in an airtight container, interleaved with greaseproof paper, in a cool place for up to 1 week.

For a two-tone decoration, use a combination of dark and white chocolate curls, applying them to the cake before the ganache or icing has set firmly, to ensure they adhere.

CHOCOLATE CURLS – THE EASY WAY
Use a 200g (7oz) bar of good quality white or dark chocolate. Melt the chocolate with a knob of butter and stir until smooth. Pour into a small rectangular container (a 250g margarine tub is ideal) and leave to cool so the chocolate hardens. Before shaping the curls, allow the chocolate to soften slightly at warm room temperature.

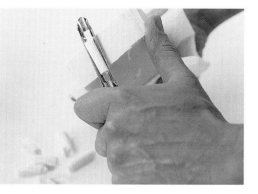

Upturn the tub of set chocolate and pop the set chocolate block out on to a marble slab or clean surface. Hold the chocolate block in a piece of kitchen paper (to prevent the warmth of your hand melting it), and use a swivel vegetable peeler to shave off curls along the length of the block. Store as for chocolate curls (see left).

CHOCOLATE CUT-OUTS

You can cut all sorts of shapes from set, melted chocolate to use as decorations for cakes and cold desserts. Use a sharp knife to cut squares, triangles or diamonds, or abstract shapes. For leaves, hearts, stars etc, use small pastry cutters. Spread a thin, even layer of melted chocolate on a marble slab or board lined with baking parchment. Leave to cool at room temperature until firm enough to cut, but not brittle.

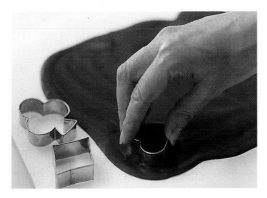

Press the cutter firmly through the chocolate to cut out the required shape.

Lift off the cutter and place the chocolate shape on the marble slab or board. Avoid touching the surface of the shapes with your fingers if possible, or you might mark them. Store the cut-out shapes in an airtight container, interleaved with greaseproof paper, in a cool place for up to 1 week.

CHOCOLATE RIBBONS

These make an impressive finish for elegant cakes; see Chocolate ribbon cake (page 124).

Cut 12 strips of baking parchment, each 30cm (12in) long and 3cm (1¼in) wide. Brush thinly with melted plain chocolate to coat evenly.

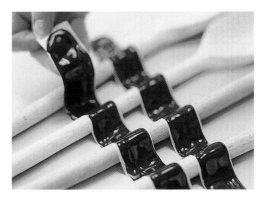

Lay the strips over parallel wooden spoon handles to make waves. Leave until set, but not brittle.

Carefully peel the paper away from the ribbons.

PIPED CHOCOLATE DECORATIONS

Fill a greaseproof paper piping bag with melted chocolate, snip off the very tip, and you can create all kinds of piped chocolate decorations.

Draw outlines on non-stick baking parchment, using a template as a guide, turn the paper over and pipe over the marked lines. Leave to set.

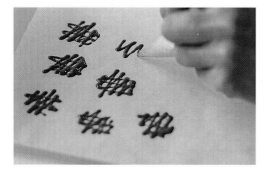

Alternatively, simply pipe freehand designs directly on to baking parchment and leave to set.

Once the decorations have set, carefully peel the parchment away from them.

Using a greaseproof paper piping bag filled with melted plain, milk or white chocolate, you can pipe effective designs directly on to a cake coated with ganache or icing. Choose a chocolate that will contrast with the colour of your cake covering; milk chocolate, for example, works well on a cake covered with dark ganache.

Snip off the merest tip from the end of the greaseproof paper piping bag. Hold it about 2.5cm (1in) above the surface of the cake and gently squeeze the bag as you move it quickly, backwards and forwards across the cake, to create a zig-zag pattern.

For a more elaborate finish, turn the cake around 180°, and overpipe the zig-zag design with a repeat pattern. Leave in a cool place until set.

CHOCOLATE LEAVES

Choose leaves with well-defined veins, such as rose leaves or bay leaves, and make sure they are thoroughly clean and dry.

Holding the leaf by the stem, paint the underside with melted chocolate, using a small paintbrush; don't let the chocolate extend over the edges.

Put the leaves, chocolate-side up, on a sheet of non-stick baking parchment and leave until set.

Carefully peel each leaf away from the chocolate.

CHOCOLATE DIPPED FRUIT

Choose small, unblemished fruits that are ripe, but firm. Strawberries, cherries, physalis fruit, kumquats and grapes are suitable. Wash the fruit if necessary, but don't remove the stems; pat dry thoroughly with kitchen paper. Use melted plain, milk or white chocolate.

Holding the fruit by the stem, partially dip it into the melted chocolate to half-coat. Lift out and allow the excess chocolate to drip back into the bowl.

Carefully put the dipped fruits on a sheet of non-stick baking parchment and leave to set. Use to decorate desserts or cakes, or serve an assortment of dipped fruits to round off a meal.

1

HOT PUDDINGS

QUICK GOOEY CHOCOLATE PUDDINGS

CHOCOLATE STEAMED SPONGE PUDDING

CHOCOLATE CRUMB PUDDING

MINI CHOCOLATE AND CHERRY PUDDINGS

DARK PUDDINGS WITH WHITE CHOCOLATE CUSTARD

BANANA AND CHOCOLATE BREAD PUDDING

CHOCOLATE PANETTONE PUDDING

GOOEY CHOCOLATE SOUFFLÉS

MOCHA SOUFFLÉS

CHOCOLATE, PRUNE AND ORANGE SOUFFLÉS

CHOCOLATE SOUFFLÉS WITH VANILLA CREAM

RASPBERRIES WITH CHOCOLATE MALLOW

DOUBLE CHOCOLATE BAKED ALASKAS

PEAR GALETTES WITH CHOCOLATE SAUCE

CHOCOLATE AND CHERRY AMARETTI TART

CHOCOLATE CRÊPES WITH A BOOZY SAUCE

CHOCOLATE AND BANANA CRÊPES

QUICK GOOEY CHOCOLATE PUDDINGS

PREPARATION TIME: 15 minutes

COOKING TIME: 12–15 minutes

PER SERVING: 480 cals; 34g fat; 40g carbohydrate

MAKES 4

100g (3½oz) butter, plus extra to grease

100g (3½oz) golden caster sugar, plus extra to dust

100g (3½oz) plain, dark chocolate with 70% cocoa
   solids, in pieces

2 large eggs

20g (¾oz) plain flour

Icing sugar to dust

Moist and spongy on the outside, soft and unctuous within, these warm, sticky puddings are totally indulgent. As you cut into your individual pudding, watch with anticipation as the dark, gooey centre trickles across the plate.

1 Preheat the oven to 200°C (180°C fan oven) mark 6. Butter four 200ml (7fl oz) ramekins and sprinkle with sugar.

2 Put the chocolate in a heatproof bowl with the butter. Melt over a pan of gently simmering water, then allow to cool for 5 minutes.

3 Whisk the eggs, caster sugar and flour together in a bowl until smooth. Fold in the chocolate mixture and pour into the ramekins.

4 Stand the dishes on a baking tray and bake for 12–15 minutes or until the puddings are puffed and set on the outside, but still runny inside. Turn out, dust with icing sugar and serve immediately.

CHOCOLATE STEAMED SPONGE PUDDING

PREPARATION TIME: 20 minutes

COOKING TIME: 1½ hours

PER SERVING: 580 cals; 32g fat; 68g carbohydrate

SERVES 4

125g (4oz) butter, plus extra to grease

4 level tbsp cocoa powder

125g (4oz) golden caster sugar

Few drops of vanilla extract

2 large eggs, beaten

175g (6oz) self-raising flour, sifted

2–4 tbsp semi-skimmed milk to mix

Reminiscent of comforting school puddings, this classic recipe is a firm, family favourite.

1 Half-fill a steamer or large saucepan with water and put it on to boil. Grease a 900ml (1½ pint) pudding basin.

2 Blend the cocoa powder with 2 tbsp hot water to a smooth cream; allow to cool. Cream the butter and sugar together in a bowl until pale and fluffy. Stir in the vanilla extract, then the cooled blended cocoa.

3 Add the beaten eggs, a little at a time, beating well after each addition. Using a metal spoon, fold in half of the sifted flour, then fold in the rest, with enough milk to give a dropping consistency.

4 Spoon the mixture into the basin. Lay a greased and pleated sheet of foil or double thick greaseproof paper over the top of the bowl and secure under the rim with string. Lower into the pan, cover tightly and steam for 1½ hours, topping up the pan with boiling water as necessary.

5 Lift out the basin and remove the foil or greaseproof paper. Turn out the pudding on to a warmed plate and serve with custard.

CHOCOLATE CRUMB PUDDING

PREPARATION TIME: 20 minutes

COOKING TIME: 1¼–1½ hours

PER SERVING: 400 cals; 23g fat; 45g carbohydrate

SERVES 4

75g (3oz) butter, plus extra to grease

50g (2oz) plain, dark chocolate with at least 60% cocoa solids, in pieces

75g (3oz) golden caster sugar

1 egg, separated

½–1 tsp vanilla extract

100g (4oz) fresh white breadcrumbs

50g (2oz) self-raising flour, sifted

4–5 tbsp semi-skimmed milk

TO SERVE

Chocolate fudge sauce (page 138)

Soft, white breadcrumbs give this steamed pudding a lovely light texture. It's served with a rich fudgy chocolate sauce poured over, for a heavenly contrast.

1 Half-fill a steamer or large saucepan with water and put it on to boil. Grease a 900ml (1½ pint) pudding basin.

2 Melt the chocolate in a heatproof bowl over a pan of simmering water; cool for 5 minutes. Cream the butter and sugar together in a bowl until pale and fluffy, then beat in the chocolate, egg yolk and vanilla extract.

3 Combine the breadcrumbs and flour and fold half into the creamed mixture, with 2 tbsp milk. Fold in the remaining breadcrumbs and flour, with sufficient milk to give a fairly soft dropping consistency. Whisk the egg white in a separate bowl to firm peaks and fold into the mixture.

4 Spoon the mixture into the basin. Lay a greased and pleated sheet of foil or double thick greaseproof paper over the top of the bowl and secure under the rim with string. Lower into the pan, cover tightly and steam for 1¼–1½ hours, topping up the pan with boiling water as necessary.

5 Take out the basin, remove the cover and turn out the pudding on to a warmed plate. Serve with the hot chocolate fudge sauce.

MINI CHOCOLATE AND CHERRY PUDDINGS

PREPARATION TIME: 35 minutes
COOKING TIME: 25–30 minutes
PER SERVING: 520 cals; 36g fat; 43g carbohydrate

SERVES 8

125g (4oz) unsalted butter, melted and cooled, plus extra
    to grease
75g (3oz) hazelnuts, plus extra to decorate
125g (4oz) plain chocolate, in pieces
4 large eggs
125g (4oz) golden caster sugar
50g (2oz) self-raising flour
1 level tbsp cocoa powder
75g (3oz) pitted morello cherries (from a jar), drained and
    halved, plus extra to decorate
Kirsch to drizzle (optional)

CHOCOLATE SAUCE

75g (3oz) plain chocolate
2 tbsp Kirsch or brandy
142ml carton double cream

Impress your family and friends with these mouthwatering puddings. To keep them really squidgy, we have used just a hint of flour. For a special treat, drizzle a dash of Kirsch over each pudding before pouring on the chocolate sauce.

1 Preheat the oven to 180°C (160°C fan oven) mark 4. Grease and base-line eight 150ml (¼ pint) dariole moulds. Preheat the grill, spread the hazelnuts in the grill pan and toast until lightly browned. Allow to cool, then chop.

2 Put the chocolate in a heatproof bowl and set over a pan of simmering water to melt. Stir until smooth, then leave to cool.

3 Beat the eggs and sugar together in a bowl until the mixture is pale and light, and has doubled in volume.

4 Sift the flour and cocoa powder together over the whisked mixture. Pour the melted butter around the edge of the bowl, then fold to combine, using a large metal spoon or spatula. Fold in the melted chocolate, chopped hazelnuts and cherries.

5 Spoon the mixture into the prepared moulds and stand them on a baking sheet. Bake in the oven for 25–30 minutes, covering lightly with foil if the tops appear to be browning too quickly.

6 Meanwhile, make the sauce. Put the chocolate, Kirsch and cream in a small pan and heat gently until smooth.

7 Turn out the puddings on to warmed serving plates and spoon 1 tsp Kirsch over each one if you like. Spoon over the chocolate sauce and top with the extra cherries and hazelnuts. Serve straightaway, with a jug of pouring cream.

TO FREEZE: Cool the puddings after baking and wrap in clingfilm. Make the sauce and cool. Freeze in separate containers for up to 3 months. Thaw both puddings and sauce at cool room temperature for 3 hours. Warm the puddings at 180°C (160°C fan oven) mark 4 for 20 minutes. Reheat the chocolate sauce in a pan. Finish and serve as above.

DARK PUDDINGS WITH WHITE CHOCOLATE CUSTARD

PREPARATION TIME: 20 minutes

COOKING TIME: 20–25 minutes

PER SERVING: 380 cals; 26g fat; 30g carbohydrate

SERVES 6

125g (4oz) butter, plus extra to grease

25g (1oz) hazelnuts

75g (3oz) dark muscovado sugar

75g (3oz) self-raising flour

½ level tsp baking powder

2 level tbsp cocoa powder, plus extra to dust

25g (1oz) plain chocolate, roughly chopped

2 large eggs, beaten

WHITE CHOCOLATE CUSTARD

4 level tsp custard powder

4 level tsp sugar

450ml (¾ pint) semi-skimmed milk

40g (1½oz) white chocolate drops

These light, airy puddings are easy to make and surprisingly low in calories – the ideal dessert if you – or any of your guests – are weight watching.

1 Preheat the oven to 180°C (160°C fan oven) mark 4. Lightly grease and base-line six 150ml (¼ pint) ramekins with non-stick baking parchment. Preheat the grill, spread the hazelnuts in the grill pan and toast until lightly browned. Allow to cool, then roughly chop.

2 Put the butter and sugar in a pan and heat gently until melted and combined. Set aside to cool.

3 Sift the flour, baking powder and cocoa powder together into a bowl. Stir in the chopped hazelnuts and chocolate, then make a well in the centre. Pour in the melted mixture and the beaten eggs. Beat well until evenly combined.

4 Pour the mixture into the ramekins and bake for 20–25 minutes or until the puddings are just firm to the touch.

5 Meanwhile, make the white chocolate custard. Put the custard powder and sugar in a bowl and mix in a little of the milk to make a smooth paste. Heat the remaining milk in a heavy-based pan until almost boiling, pour on to the custard mix, stirring, then return to the pan. Add the white chocolate drops and cook, stirring, until the chocolate has melted and the custard thickened.

6 Leave the puddings to stand for a minute or two, then turn out. Trim the top from each pudding, using a sharp knife; then invert on to warmed deep serving plates. Whisk the custard until foaming, then pour around the puddings. Dust with cocoa powder and serve immediately.

TO PREPARE AHEAD: Bake the puddings up to a day ahead, allow to cool, then store in an airtight container. To reheat, put the puddings on a baking sheet; cover with foil and put in the oven at 170°C (fan oven 150°C) mark 3 for 5–10 minutes. Finish and serve as above.

BANANA AND CHOCOLATE BREAD PUDDING

PREPARATION TIME: 15 minutes, plus standing
COOKING TIME: 50 minutes
PER SERVING: 730 cals; 43g fat; 76g carbohydrate

SERVES 6

225g (8oz) crustless white bread
Butter to grease
2 bananas
4 eggs
175g (6oz) golden caster sugar
284ml carton double cream
300ml (½ pint) semi-skimmed milk
2 tsp vanilla extract
½ level tsp ground cinnamon
150g (5oz) plain chocolate, roughly chopped
50g (2oz) shelled pecan nuts, roughly chopped

This is a classic New Orleans pudding. It features bananas, which are popular in the Deep South, pecan nuts that are grown there, and chunks of dark chocolate for richness. You can, of course, use other nuts – such as walnuts or macadamia nuts – or omit them altogether if you prefer.

1 Cut the bread into bite-size cubes and spread out on a board. Leave to dry out for at least 4 hours.

2 Preheat the oven to 190°C (170°C fan oven) mark 5. Butter a 2 litre (3½ pint) shallow ovenproof dish.

3 Mash the bananas in a bowl, using a fork, then beat in the eggs. Stir in the caster sugar, double cream, milk, vanilla extract and ground cinnamon. Fold the chopped chocolate and pecan nuts into the mixture with the bread cubes, then pour into the prepared dish.

4 Bake the pudding in the oven for 50 minutes or until the top is firm and golden brown. Leave to stand for about 10 minutes to allow the custard to firm up slightly. Spoon into warmed serving bowls and serve with cream or vanilla ice cream.

TO PREPARE AHEAD: Bake the pudding up to a day ahead, allow to cool, then cover and refrigerate. Reheat the puddings in the oven at 190°C (fan oven 170°C) mark 5 for about 15 minutes.

CHOCOLATE PANETTONE PUDDING

PREPARATION TIME: 30 minutes, plus standing
COOKING TIME: 1–1¼ hours
PER SERVING: 710 cals; 30g fat; 91g carbohydrate

SERVES 8

125g (4oz) raisins
100ml (3½fl oz) brandy
75g (3oz) softened butter, plus extra to grease
700g (1½lb) panettone
2 x 500 g cartons fresh custard, or 700 ml (1½ pints)
   homemade
600ml (1 pint) semi-skimmed milk
200g (7oz) plain chocolate, roughly chopped
Icing sugar to dust

Panettone, the Italian, dome-shaped Christmas yeast cake, gives this creamy bread and butter pudding a wonderful festive taste. Flavoured with sultanas, orange and citrus peel, it's available from supermarkets and delicatessens, especially around Christmas. If unobtainable, use brioche (preferably one-day old) instead.

1 Put the raisins in a bowl, pour on the brandy, cover and leave to soak overnight.

2 Preheat the oven to 180°C (160°C fan oven) mark 4 and grease a 3.4 litre (6 pint) ovenproof dish.

3 Slice the panettone into rounds, about 5mm/¼in thick. Spread with the butter and cut the slices into quarters. Stir the custard and milk together and pour a thin layer over the base of the prepared dish. Arrange a layer of panettone on top and scatter over some of the raisins and chocolate. Pour on another thin layer of custard.

4 Continue to layer up the panettone, raisins, chocolate and custard, finishing with a layer of custard. Leave to rest for 1 hour.

5 Stand the dish in a roasting tin and pour hot water around the dish to come halfway up the sides. Bake in the oven for 1–1¼ hours or until the custard is set and the top has turned a deep brown, covering lightly with foil after 40 minutes to prevent overbrowning.

6 Dust the surface lightly with icing sugar to serve.

TO FREEZE: Freeze the pudding at the end of step 4. To use, thaw overnight in the fridge, then bake and serve as above.

GOOEY CHOCOLATE SOUFFLÉS

PREPARATION TIME: 10 minutes
COOKING TIME: 12–15 minutes
PER SERVING: 110 cals; 2g fat; 18g carbohydrate

SERVES 8

125g (4oz) golden caster sugar

50g (2oz) cocoa powder

9 egg whites, at room temperature

Pinch of cream of tartar

15g (½oz) plain, dark chocolate with 60–70% cocoa
    solids, coarsely grated or finely chopped

2 tsp dark rum

1 tsp vanilla extract

Light, airy soufflés that are very quick, and easier to make than you'd imagine. They are a treat for anyone on a low-fat diet.

1 Preheat the oven to 180°C (160°C fan oven) mark 4. Sift 100g (3½oz) caster sugar together with the cocoa; put to one side.
2 Using an electric whisk, whisk the egg whites with the cream of tartar until foamy. Continue whisking at high speed, gradually adding the remaining sugar a spoonful at a time, until the meringue holds stiff peaks.
3 Using a large metal spoon, carefully fold the sugar and cocoa mixture into the meringue with the chocolate, rum and vanilla extract. The mixture should be evenly combined but still stiff.
4 Divide the mixture among eight 175ml (6fl oz) ovenproof tea or coffee cups. Stand the cups in a large roasting tin and pour enough boiling water into the tin to come at least halfway up their sides. Bake for 12–15 minutes or until puffed and set round the edges but still soft in the centre. Serve at once.

MOCHA SOUFFLÉS

PREPARATION TIME: 15 minutes
COOKING TIME: 12 minutes
PER SERVING: 140 cals; 6g fat; 17g carbohydrate

SERVES 6

50g (2oz) plain, dark chocolate with 60–70% cocoa
    solids, roughly chopped

2 level tbsp cornflour

1 level tbsp cocoa powder

1–1½ level tsp instant coffee granules

4 level tbsp golden caster sugar

150ml (¼ pint) skimmed milk

2 egg yolks

3 egg whites

Cocoa powder to dust

These tempting soufflés provide only 145 calories per serving – a great way to get your chocolate fix without spoiling your diet.

1 Preheat the oven to 190°C (170°C fan oven) mark 5 and put a baking sheet inside, to heat up.
2 Put the chocolate in a non-stick saucepan with the cornflour, cocoa powder, coffee granules, 1 level tbsp caster sugar and the milk. Warm gently, stirring over a low heat, until the chocolate has melted. Increase the heat and cook, stirring continuously, until the mixture just thickens. Leave to cool a little, then stir in the egg yolks. Cover the surface with a piece of damp greaseproof paper and allow to cool.
3 Whisk the egg whites in a clean bowl until they form soft peaks. Gradually whisk in the remaining caster sugar, a spoonful at a time, until the meringue is stiff but not dry.
4 Stir a third of the meringue into the cooled chocolate mixture to lighten it, then gently fold in the remainder, using a large metal spoon. Divide the mixture between six 150ml (¼ pint) ramekins. Stand them on the hot baking sheet and bake for about 12 minutes until puffed up.
5 Dust the soufflés with cocoa powder and serve immediately.

CHOCOLATE, PRUNE AND ORANGE SOUFFLÉS

PREPARATION TIME: 20 minutes

COOKING TIME: 15–20 minutes

PER SERVING: 150 cals; 5g fat; 26g carbohydrate

MAKES 8

Butter to grease

5 level tbsp golden caster sugar

175g (6oz) pitted, ready-to-eat prunes

2 tbsp vegetable oil

5 tbsp unsweetened orange juice

50g (2oz) plain chocolate, chopped into small pieces

Grated zest of 1 orange

5 egg whites

¼ level tsp cream of tartar

Pinch of salt

Icing sugar to dust

Complement these soufflés with a few brandied prunes (see below).

1 Preheat the oven to 180°C (160°C fan oven) mark 4. Lightly grease eight 150ml (¼ pint) ramekins and sprinkle with 1 tbsp of the caster sugar.

2 Put the prunes, vegetable oil and orange juice in a blender and whiz for 2–3 minutes to form a purée. Transfer to a large bowl and stir in the chocolate, 2 tbsp of the remaining caster sugar and the orange zest.

3 Put the egg whites, cream of tartar and salt in a clean bowl and whisk until stiff but not dry. Add the remaining 2 tbsp sugar and continue to whisk until the mixture becomes very stiff and shiny.

4 Using a large metal spoon, stir a quarter of the egg whites into the prune mixture, then gently fold in the remainder. Spoon into the ramekins.

5 Stand them in a roasting tin and add enough hot water to come halfway up the sides. Bake for 15–20 minutes or until the soufflés are just set. Dust with icing sugar and serve immediately, with brandied prunes if you like.

BRANDIED PRUNES: Put 225g (8oz) ready-to-eat prunes in a jar, pour on 200ml (7fl oz) brandy, cover with a lid or clingfilm and leave for 2–3 days.

CHOCOLATE SOUFFLÉS WITH VANILLA CREAM

PREPARATION TIME: 30 minutes
COOKING TIME: 8–10 minutes
PER SERVING: 490 cals; 41g fat; 23g carbohydrate

SERVES 8

VANILLA CREAM

300ml (½ pint) double cream
½ vanilla pod, split
2 egg yolks
25g (1oz) golden caster sugar

SOUFFLÉ

225g (8oz) plain chocolate, in pieces
15g (½oz) butter, melted
2 level tbsp cocoa powder
150ml (¼ pint) double cream
3 eggs, separated
2 tbsp rum or brandy
Pinch of cream of tartar
25g (1oz) golden caster sugar

TO SERVE

Cocoa powder, to dust

These delectable soufflés come with a surprise centre of melting chocolate. Leave them to stand for 10 minutes after cooking – this makes it easier to turn them out and doesn't spoil the texture.

1 First make the vanilla cream: Pour 150ml (¼ pint) of the cream into a heavy-based saucepan, add the vanilla pod and bring just to the boil. Remove from the heat and cool slightly. Mix the egg yolks and sugar together in a bowl. Pour in the warm cream and stir until combined. Return to the rinsed-out saucepan and cook over a low heat, stirring continuously with a wooden spoon, until the custard thickens enough to lightly coat the back of the spoon; this will take 4–5 minutes. Do not boil or the mixture will curdle. Immediately strain the vanilla cream into a cold bowl, cover and allow to cool, then chill.

2 For the soufflé, melt 75g (3oz) of the chocolate in a heatproof bowl over a pan of gently simmering water. Fill 8 cubes of an ice-cube tray with the melted chocolate. Cool, then put in the freezer to set.

3 Brush the insides of eight 7.5cm (3in) ramekins, about 5cm (2in) high, with the melted butter. Dust the insides with a little of the sifted cocoa, gently tapping out any excess. Chill the ramekins.

4 Preheat the oven to 230°C (210°C fan oven) mark 8. Put the remaining chocolate, cocoa powder and cream in a saucepan and stir over a gentle heat until the chocolate has melted and the mixture is smooth. Allow to cool slightly, then beat in the egg yolks and rum.

5 Put the egg whites and cream of tartar in a clean bowl and whisk until stiff. Gradually add the sugar and continue to whisk until the meringue is very stiff and shiny. Using a large metal spoon, carefully fold the meringue into the chocolate mixture until evenly combined.

6 Put a baking sheet in the oven to heat. Turn out the frozen chocolate cubes: Half fill the ramekins with the soufflé mixture and put a frozen chocolate cube in the centre of each. Cover with the remaining mixture and run a sharp knife around the edge of each dish to encourage an even rise. Stand the ramekins on the hot baking sheet and cook for 8–10 minutes until well risen and firm to the touch. Allow to stand for 10 minutes.

7 Pour the vanilla cream into a large saucepan and warm over a low heat. Gradually add the remaining cream, whisking with an electric whisk until the custard becomes frothy; do not boil.

8 To serve, run a round-bladed knife around the edge of the soufflés and turn out on to serving plates. Pour the vanilla cream around the soufflés, dust with cocoa powder and serve immediately.

TO PREPARE AHEAD: Make the vanilla cream to the end of step 1; refrigerate for up to 2 hours. Continue as above.

RASPBERRIES WITH CHOCOLATE MALLOW

PREPARATION TIME: 15 minutes

COOKING TIME: 20–25 minutes

PER SERVING: 120 cals; 1g fat; 27g carbohydrate

SERVES 6

225g (8oz) raspberries

Grated zest of ½ orange

125g (4oz) golden caster sugar, plus 1 level tbsp

3 large egg whites

1 level tbsp cocoa powder, sifted

15g (½oz) hazelnuts, toasted and roughly chopped

Deceptively chocolatey and rich, this tempting dessert is low in calories and contains very little fat…a slimmer's dream.

1 Preheat oven to 150°C (130°C fan oven) mark 2. Divide the raspberries, orange zest and 1 level tbsp sugar among six 150ml (¼ pint) ramekins.

2 Put the egg whites in a heatproof bowl with the 125g (4oz) caster sugar. Stand the bowl over a saucepan of gently simmering water and whisk, using an electric hand whisk, until the mixture is very stiff and shiny. Remove the bowl from the heat and whisk for 4–5 minutes or until the bowl is cool. At the last moment, fold in the cocoa powder.

3 Spoon the meringue over the fruit and sprinkle the chopped hazelnuts on top. Bake for 20–25 minutes or until the meringue is lightly coloured, crisp on the outside and soft in the middle. Serve immediately.

DOUBLE CHOCOLATE BAKED ALASKAS

PREPARATION TIME: 20 minutes, plus freezing

COOKING TIME: 5 minutes

PER SERVING: 630 cals; 30g fat; 84g carbohydrate

SERVES 6

200g (7oz) plain chocolate digestive biscuits

50g (2oz) melted butter, plus extra to grease

600ml (1 pint) good quality chocolate ice cream

2 chocolate flake bars, roughly chopped

4 large egg whites

225g (8oz) golden caster sugar

50g (2oz) desiccated coconut

TO FINISH

Cocoa powder to dust

Toasted coconut shavings (optional)

An impressive, easy pudding, that can be prepared well ahead, ready to pop into the oven minutes before serving.

1 Finely crush the biscuits, then stir in the hot, melted butter. Using a 6cm (2½in) pastry cutter as a template, press the mixture into 6 rounds on a lightly greased baking sheet and freeze for 30 minutes.

2 Beat the ice cream to soften it slightly and pile into mounds on the biscuit bases. Make a shallow hollow in the centre of each ice cream mound and fill with the chopped chocolate flakes. Return to the freezer for at least 1 hour until firm.

3 Put the egg whites and sugar in a large bowl set over a pan of barely simmering water. Using an electric whisk, beat for 10 minutes or until the mixture is thick and glossy. Fold in the desiccated coconut. Allow to cool for 5 minutes.

4 Cover the ice cream mounds completely with a thick layer of meringue. Return to the freezer for at least 4 hours or overnight.

5 To serve, preheat the oven to 220°C (200°C fan oven) mark 7, then bake the puddings for 5 minutes or until golden. Dust with cocoa powder, top with toasted coconut if you like, and serve immediately.

PEAR GALETTES WITH CHOCOLATE SAUCE

PREPARATION TIME: 15 minutes
COOKING TIME: 6–8 minutes
PER SERVING: 320 cals; 14g fat; 47g carbohydrate

MAKES 6

1 tube ready-to-bake pain au chocolat dough with
    chocolate pieces (see cook's tip)
Flour to dust
2 firm, ripe pears
Ground cinnamon to sprinkle
6 level tsp dark muscovado sugar
150ml (¼ pint) semi-skimmed milk

TO FINISH
Ground cinnamon to sprinkle
Icing sugar to dust

Pears have a natural affinity with chocolate and these attractive little galettes are easy to make, using ready-to-bake dough.

1 Preheat the oven at 200°C (180°C fan oven) mark 6 and put a baking sheet in the oven to heat. Unroll the pain au chocolat dough on to a lightly floured work surface; set aside the chocolate pieces. Using a cup or saucer as a guide, cut out 6 circles of dough, about 10cm (4in) in diameter. Put these on a second (cold) baking sheet.

2 Quarter the pears and cut out the cores; peel them too, if you prefer. Thickly slice the pear quarters.

3 Arrange the pear slices on top of the dough circles, in a spiral fashion radiating out from the centre. Sprinkle each one with a little ground cinnamon and 1 level tsp muscovado sugar.

4 Slide the baking sheet on to the hot baking sheet in the oven. Bake for 6–8 minutes or until the galettes are golden brown.

5 Meanwhile, make the chocolate sauce. Bring the milk to the boil in a saucepan, then whisk in the reserved chocolate pieces. Bubble for about 3 minutes or until the sauce is syrupy.

6 Dust the pear galettes with a little ground cinnamon and icing sugar, as soon as you take them out of the oven. Serve straightaway, with the warm chocolate sauce.

COOK'S TIP: Tubes of pain au chocolat dough are available from supermarkets. If you cannot find them, use 350g (12oz) ready-made puff pastry and 40g (1½oz) plain, dark chocolate, broken into small pieces. Roll out the puff pastry and complete the recipe as above, cooking at the same temperature but for 20 minutes.

CHOCOLATE AND CHERRY AMARETTI TART

PREPARATION TIME: 30 minutes, plus chilling
COOKING TIME: About 1¼ hours, plus cooling
PER SERVING: 760 cals; 49g fat; 68g carbohydrate

SERVES 8

400g (14oz) pitted bottled or canned morello cherries, drained
3 tbsp brandy, sloe gin or Amaretto liqueur

PASTRY
150g (5oz) butter, softened
50g (2oz) icing sugar
1 small egg, beaten
225g (8oz) plain flour, sifted, plus extra to dust

FILLING
100g (3½oz) plain chocolate, in pieces
50g (2oz) amaretti biscuits
125g (4oz) butter, softened
125g (4oz) golden caster sugar
3 large eggs, beaten
125g (4oz) ground almonds
25g (1oz) self-raising flour
75g (3oz) slivered or flaked almonds

TO FINISH
Icing sugar to dust

Chocolate and cherries are a classic combination, and morello cherries give this chocolate and almond tart a wonderful depth of flavour. There are several brands available, in both jars and cans.

1 Put the morello cherries in a bowl, pour on the brandy, sloe gin or liqueur, cover and set aside for 30 minutes to allow the flavours to develop.

2 Meanwhile, make the pastry. Put the butter, icing sugar and egg in a food processor and whiz until almost smooth. Add the flour and process until the mixture just begins to form a dough. Turn out on to a lightly floured work surface, knead the pastry gently, then wrap in clingfilm and chill for 30 minutes.

3 Roll out the pastry on a lightly floured surface and use to line a 24cm (9½in) fluted, loose-bottomed flan tin. Chill for 20 minutes.

4 Preheat the oven to 200°C (180°C fan oven) mark 6. Line the pastry case with greaseproof paper and baking beans and bake 'blind' for 15 minutes. Remove the paper and beans and return the pastry case to the oven for a further 5 minutes to cook the base. Lower the oven setting to 150°C (130°C fan oven) mark 2.

5 To make the filling, melt the plain chocolate in a heatproof bowl over a pan of simmering water. Stir until smooth, then set aside to cool. Crush the amaretti biscuits finely. In a bowl, beat together the butter and sugar until pale and fluffy. Gradually beat in the eggs, alternately with the ground almonds and flour. Finally, fold in the cooled melted chocolate and crushed amaretti.

6 Spoon about one third of the mixture over the base of the pastry case. Spoon the cherries evenly over the surface, then top with the remaining filling mixture and spread out carefully to cover the cherries. Sprinkle the almonds over the surface and bake in the oven for about 1 hour. The tart will have a thin crust on top, but be quite soft underneath.

7 Leave the tart in the tin for 10–15 minutes to firm up, then carefully unmould and dust with icing sugar. Serve warm.

TO PREPARE AHEAD: Prepare and bake the tart (to the end of step 6). Leave in the tin, cover loosely with greaseproof paper and store at room temperature for up to 24 hours. To serve, cover the tart loosely with foil and warm at 200°C (180°C fan oven) mark 6 for 10 minutes. Dust with icing sugar to serve.

TO FREEZE: Prepare the tart to the end of step 6, then cool, wrap and freeze. To use, thaw at cool room temperature overnight. Warm through at 200°C (180°C fan oven) mark 6 for 10 minutes and dust with icing sugar before serving.

CHOCOLATE CRÊPES WITH A BOOZY SAUCE

PREPARATION TIME: 5 minutes, plus standing
COOKING TIME: 10 minutes
PER SERVING: 550 cals; 32g fat; 52g carbohydrate

SERVES 4

100g (3½oz) plain flour, sifted
Pinch of salt
1 medium egg
300ml (½ pint) semi-skimmed milk
Sunflower oil for frying
100g (3½oz) unsalted butter
100g (3½oz) light muscovado sugar, plus extra to sprinkle
4 tbsp brandy
50g (2oz) plain, dark chocolate with 70% cocoa solids, roughly chopped

Sumptuous chocolate-filled pancakes, bathed in a brandy sauce.

1 Put the flour and salt in a food processor. Add the egg and milk and process until smooth. Pour the batter into a jug, cover and leave to stand for about 20 minutes.

2 Heat 1 tsp oil in a 23cm (9in) non-stick crêpe pan or frying pan. Pour in 100ml (3½fl oz) batter, tilting the pan around so the batter coats the base, and cook for 1–2 minutes until golden underneath. Use a palette knife to flip the crêpe over, and cook the other side.

3 Tip the crêpe on to a plate, cover with a piece of greaseproof paper and repeat with the remaining batter, using a little more oil as necessary, and stacking the crêpes as they are cooked.

4 Melt the butter and sugar together in a frying pan over a low heat. Add the brandy and stir.

5 Divide the chocolate between the crêpes. Fold each in half, then in half again. Slide each one into the frying pan and cook for 3–4 minutes to melt the chocolate, turning halfway through to coat with the sauce. Serve the crêpes drizzled with the sauce and sprinkled with extra sugar.

CHOCOLATE AND BANANA CRÊPES

PREPARATION TIME: 15 minutes, plus chilling
COOKING TIME: 30–40 minutes
PER SERVING: 590 cals; 22g fat; 75g carbohydrate

SERVES 4

150g (5oz) plain chocolate
100g (3½oz) plain flour
1 large egg
Pinch of salt
300ml (½ pint) semi-skimmed milk
25g (1oz) butter
1 level tbsp light muscovado sugar
4 medium bananas, thickly sliced
120ml (4fl oz) brandy
Sunflower oil for frying
Icing sugar to dust

These pancakes are divine served with ice cream. To ring the changes, use other fruit, such as pineapple, instead of bananas.

1 Chop the chocolate in a food processor; take out half of it and set aside. Add the flour, egg, salt and milk to the chocolate in the processor and whiz until smooth. Pour the batter into a jug, cover and chill for 30 minutes.

2 Melt the butter and sugar in a frying pan. Add the bananas and stir-fry over a medium heat for 3 minutes. Add the brandy (carefully, as it may ignite in the pan). Continue to simmer for about 2 minutes until the bananas soften and the liquid is syrupy; set aside.

3 Brush an 18cm (7in) non-stick crêpe pan or small frying pan with oil and heat. Stir the batter, then pour about 4 tbsp into the pan to coat the base thinly. Cook for 2 minutes or until golden brown. Flip the crêpe over and cook the other side for 1 minute. Transfer to a plate and keep warm. Repeat with the remaining batter.

4 Put two spoonfuls of banana filling on one half of each crêpe and scatter the reserved chocolate on top. Fold in half, then in half again; keep warm while filling the remaining crêpes. Dust with icing sugar and serve.

2

COLD DESSERTS

RICH CHOCOLATE POTS

CHOCOLATE MOUSSE

BOOZY PANNA COTTA

BAKED CHOCOLATE AND COFFEE CUSTARDS

WHITE CHOCOLATE AND RED FRUIT TRIFLE

VANILLA TIRAMISU

COLD CHOCOLATE SOUFFLÉ

RICH CHOCOLATE TERRINE WITH VANILLA SAUCE

LAYERED CHOCOLATE MOUSSE CAKE TERRINE

ORANGE AND CHOCOLATE CHEESECAKE

BAKED RICOTTA TORTE

RASPBERRY AND WHITE CHOCOLATE TARTS

STRAWBERRY CHOCOLATE TART

ALMOND AND WHITE CHOCOLATE TART

CHOCOLATE AND HAZELNUT TART

CHOCOLATE AND ORANGE TRUFFLE TORTE

PROFITEROLES

CHOCOLATE CROQUEMBOUCHE

CHESTNUT AND CHOCOLATE MACAROON

HAZELNUT MERINGUE GÂTEAU

STRAWBERRY AND CHOCOLATE PAVLOVA

CHOCOLATE AND HAZELNUT MERINGUES

CHOCOLATE MERINGUE ROULADE

BLACK FOREST ROULADE

CHOCOLATE AND PRUNE ROULADE

SPICY POACHED PEARS WITH CHOCOLATE SAUCE

CHOCOLATE CINNAMON SORBET

CHOCOLATE ICE CREAM

TIRAMISU ICE CREAM

MOCHA ICE CREAM

RICH CHOCOLATE POTS

PREPARATION TIME: 15 minutes, plus chilling
PER SERVING: 800 cals; 67g fat; 46g carbohydrate

SERVES 6

300g (11oz) plain chocolate, in pieces
284ml carton double cream
250g tub mascarpone
3 tbsp cognac
1 tbsp vanilla extract

TO DECORATE

6 level tbsp crème fraîche
Chocolate curls (see page 10)

An elegant, rich chocolate indulgence…no better way to round off a gourmet feast. Use a good quality plain chocolate, such as Bournville, but not a very dark variety, otherwise the flavour of the chocolate pots will be too bitter.

1 Put the chocolate in a heatproof bowl over a pan of gently simmering water. Leave until melted, then stir until smooth. Remove the bowl from the heat.
2 Add the cream, mascarpone, cognac and vanilla extract, and mix well together – the hot chocolate will melt the mascarpone.
3 Divide the mixture between six 150ml (¼ pint) glasses and chill for about 20 minutes.
4 Spoon a dollop of crème fraîche on top of each dessert and decorate with chocolate curls. Serve with cigarettes russes biscuits.

CHOCOLATE MOUSSE

PREPARATION TIME: 20 minutes, plus chilling
PER SERVING: 380 cals; 21g fat; 36g carbohydrate

SERVES 8

350g (12oz) plain chocolate, in pieces
6 tbsp rum, brandy or cold black coffee
6 large eggs, separated
Pinch of salt
Chocolate curls (see page 10), to decorate

This rich mousse is best made with a good quality plain chocolate, such as Bournville, for a smooth, creamy flavour. Avoid using a very dark chocolate with a high percentage of cocoa solids, as the flavour of the mousse would be too bitter.

1 Put the chocolate in a bowl over a pan of barely simmering water with the rum, brandy or black coffee. Leave to melt, stirring occasionally. Remove from the heat and let cool slightly for 3–4 minutes, stirring frequently.
2 Beat the egg yolks with 2 tbsp water, then beat into the chocolate mixture until evenly blended.
3 Whisk the egg whites with the salt in a clean bowl until firm peaks form, then fold into the chocolate mixture.
4 Pour the mixture into a 1.4–1.7 litre (2½–3 pint) soufflé dish or divide between eight 150 ml (¼ pint) ramekins. Chill in the refrigerator for at least 4 hours, or overnight, until set.

BOOZY PANNA COTTA

PREPARATION TIME: 20 minutes, plus chilling
PER SERVING: 670 cals; 46g fat; 49g carbohydrate

SERVES 2

142ml carton double cream

150ml (¼ pint) semi-skimmed milk

3 level tbsp light muscovado sugar

1 level tbsp instant espresso coffee powder

50ml (2fl oz) Tia Maria or other coffee liqueur

40g (1½oz) plain, dark chocolate with 70% cocoa solids, chopped

1½ level tsp powdered gelatine

1 tsp vanilla extract

4 chocolate-coated coffee beans (optional)

Laced with coffee liqueur, this rich, creamy dessert is the perfect way to round off a romantic dinner for two.

1 Oil two 150ml (¼ pint) individual pudding basins and line them with clingfilm.

2 Put 100ml (3½fl oz) cream into a small pan with the milk, sugar, coffee, 1 tbsp liqueur and the chocolate. Heat gently until the chocolate has melted, then bring to the boil.

3 Take off the heat, sprinkle the gelatine over the surface and leave for 5 minutes. Stir well to ensure the gelatine is fully dissolved, then add the vanilla extract and mix well. Strain the mixture through a sieve into a jug, then pour into the lined basins and chill for 2 hours.

4 To serve, unmould the panna cottas on to plates and remove clingfilm. Stir the rest of the liqueur into the remaining cream and drizzle around the panna cottas. Top with chocolate-coated coffee beans if you like.

BAKED CHOCOLATE AND COFFEE CUSTARDS

PREPARATION TIME: 15 minutes, plus chilling
COOKING TIME: 20–25 minutes
PER SERVING: 460 cals; 36g fat; 31g carbohydrate

SERVES 6

CUSTARDS
284ml carton semi-skimmed milk
142ml carton double cream
200g (7oz) plain chocolate, broken into small pieces
4 large egg yolks
1 level tbsp golden caster sugar
3 tbsp very strong cold black coffee

TOPPING
125g (4oz) mascarpone
1 level tsp icing sugar
Grated zest and juice of ½ orange

TO DECORATE (optional)
Grated orange zest

These individual mocha custards are equally delicious flavoured with rum or brandy in place of the coffee. They are easy to make, and can be prepared a day ahead. Serve them with crisp, thin shortbread biscuits, for a contrast in texture.

1 Preheat the oven to 170°C (150°C fan oven) mark 3. Put the milk, cream and chocolate in a heavy-based pan over a very gentle heat until melted. Stir until smooth.

2 Mix the egg yolks, sugar and coffee together in a bowl, then pour on the warm chocolate milk. Briefly mix together, then strain through a sieve into a jug. Pour the mixture into six 150ml (¼ pint) ovenproof custard cups or ramekins.

3 Stand the dishes in a large roasting tin containing enough hot water to come halfway up their sides. Bake in the oven for 20–25 minutes or until just set and still a little wobbly in the middle – they'll firm up as they cool. Carefully lift the dishes out of the roasting tin and leave to cool, then stand on a small tray and chill for at least 3 hours.

4 To make the topping, beat the mascarpone, icing sugar, orange zest and juice together until smooth. Cover and chill for 1–2 hours.

5 To serve, put a spoonful of the mascarpone mixture on top of each custard, and decorate with grated orange zest if you like. Serve with thin shortbread biscuits.

TO PREPARE AHEAD: Bake the custards and allow to cool. Make the topping and cover the bowl. Cover the ramekins with clingfilm and refrigerate, with the topping, for up to 24 hours. Serve as above.

WHITE CHOCOLATE AND RED FRUIT TRIFLE

PREPARATION TIME: 45 minutes, plus chilling
COOKING TIME: 15 minutes
PER SERVING (FOR 8): 930 cals; 64g fat; 79g carbohydrate
PER SERVING (FOR 10): 740 cals; 51g fat; 63g carbohydrate

SERVES 8–10

3 x 500g bags frozen mixed berries
125g (4oz) golden caster sugar, plus 1 level tsp
250g (9oz) biscotti or cantuccini biscuits
5 tbsp dessert wine or fruit juice (eg cranberry and orange)

WHITE CHOCOLATE TOPPING
450ml (¾ pint) double cream
200g (7oz) good quality white chocolate, broken into pieces
500g carton fresh custard (at room temperature)
500ml carton crème fraîche

In this trifle with a modern twist, summer berries cut through the richness of the white chocolate custard beautifully. Make it a day ahead so the flavours have time to develop.

1 Put the mixed berries in a large pan with 125g (4oz) caster sugar, and heat gently for about 5 minutes until the sugar has dissolved and the berries have thawed.

2 Tip the berry mixture into a sieve over a bowl to catch the juices. Return the juices to the pan, then tip the berries into the bowl.

3 Bring the juices to the boil and simmer for about 10 minutes or until reduced to about 150ml (¼ pint). Pour over the berries and leave to cool.

4 Lay the biscotti over the base of a 3 litre (5¼ pint) trifle dish, or individual glass dishes, and sprinkle with the dessert wine or fruit juice. Scatter the cooled berries over the top.

5 For the topping, lightly whip the cream. Transfer half of it to another bowl, cover and put in the fridge; leave the remainder at room temperature. Melt the white chocolate in a bowl over a pan of barely simmering water, stirring occasionally.

6 Pour the melted chocolate into a cold bowl, at the same time gradually folding in the custard. Fold in the whipped cream at room temperature. (Doing it in this order stops the chocolate separating.) Pour the white chocolate custard over the fruit to cover it evenly.

7 Beat the crème fraîche until smooth, fold in the reserved chilled whipped cream and extra sugar, then spoon over the custard. Chill for 2 hours. Remove the trifle from the fridge 20 minutes before serving.

COOK'S TIPS
• Bags of frozen mixed berry fruits are available from supermarkets.
• Remember to remove the carton of custard from the fridge 20 minutes before you start to make the trifle, to bring it to room temperature.

VANILLA TIRAMISU

PREPARATION TIME: 20 minutes, plus chilling
PER SERVING: 380 cals; 27g fat; 27g carbohydrate

SERVES 10

200g tub mascarpone

1 vanilla pod

450ml (¾ pint) warm, strong black coffee

4 medium egg yolks

75g (3oz) golden caster sugar

284ml carton double cream

100ml (4fl oz) grappa

200g packet Savoiardi or sponge fingers

1 level tbsp cocoa powder to dust

Tiramisu is deceptively easy to make and this version is gorgeous! It also improves in flavour if you make it a day in advance.

1. Put the mascarpone into a bowl. Split the vanilla pod in half lengthways, scrape out the seeds and add them to the mascarpone.
2. Pour the coffee into a shallow dish, add the vanilla pod and set aside to allow the flavours to mingle.
3. In a large bowl, whisk the egg yolks and sugar together until pale and thick, then whisk in the mascarpone until smooth.
4. Whip the cream in another bowl to soft peaks, then fold into the mascarpone mixture with the grappa.
5. Take half of the sponge fingers and dip each in turn into the coffee mixture, then arrange over the base of a 2.4 litre (4½ pint) shallow dish. Spread a layer of mascarpone mixture over the sponge fingers, then dip the remaining sponge fingers into the coffee and arrange on top. Finish with a final layer of mascarpone. Cover and chill for at least 2 hours.
6. Dust with cocoa and cut into individual portions, using a sharp knife. Use a spatula to lift the tiramisu portions neatly on to individual plates.

COLD CHOCOLATE SOUFFLÉ

PREPARATION TIME: 20 minutes, plus chilling
PER SERVING: 650 cals; 51g fat; 36g carbohydrate

SERVES 4

3 large eggs, separated

75g (3oz) golden caster sugar

75g (3oz) plain, dark chocolate with 60–70% cocoa
   solids, in pieces

1 level tbsp powdered gelatine

1 tbsp brandy

284ml carton double cream

TO FINISH

Chocolate curls (see page 10), or coarsely grated
   chocolate

A cold soufflé set high above the rim of the dish always looks impressive, yet it isn't difficult to achieve. It's important to use the correct size of dish, to ensure the mixture sets above the rim, so both volume and diameter measurements are given below.

1 Prepare a 600ml (1 pint) soufflé dish, 12cm (5in) diameter. Cut a double strip of greaseproof paper long enough to go around the soufflé dish with the ends overlapping slightly, and deep enough to reach from the bottom of the dish to about 7cm (2¾in) above the rim. Wrap the paper around the dish and secure under the rim with string or an elastic band, so that it fits closely to the top of the dish.

2 Whisk the egg yolks and sugar together in a deep heatproof bowl over a pan of hot water, until thick and creamy. Remove from the heat and continue whisking from time to time until cool.

3 Meanwhile, melt the chocolate in a heatproof bowl over a pan of simmering water; stir until smooth and allow to cool slightly.

4 Put 2 tbsp water in a small bowl, sprinkle the gelatine over the surface and leave to soften for 10 minutes. Stand this bowl over a small pan of simmering water until the gelatine is dissolved. Allow it to cool slightly, then pour it into the egg mixture in a steady stream, stirring all the time.

5 Stir in the melted chocolate with the brandy. Allow the mixture to cool until it is almost at the point of setting.

6 Lightly whip half the cream and fold it into the chocolate mixture. Whisk the egg whites in a clean bowl until stiff but not dry, then quickly and lightly fold them into the mixture, using a large metal spoon, until evenly incorporated. Pour at once into the prepared soufflé dish and chill for 2–3 hours until set.

7 To serve, once the soufflé has set, remove the string or elastic band and ease the paper away from the soufflé with a knife dipped in hot water. Whip the rest of the cream until thick and put 6–8 neat dollops around the top edge of the soufflé. Top with chocolate curls or grated chocolate.

RICH CHOCOLATE TERRINE WITH VANILLA SAUCE

PREPARATION TIME: 45 minutes, plus cooling and overnight chilling
COOKING TIME: 1¾ hours
PER SERVING: 500 cals; 38g fat; 27g carbohydrate

SERVES 12

CHOCOLATE TERRINE

Oil to grease
350g (12oz) plain, dark chocolate with 70% cocoa solids, broken into small pieces
40g (1½oz) cocoa powder
6 large eggs, beaten
125g (4oz) light muscovado sugar
284ml carton double cream
5 tbsp brandy (optional)

VANILLA SAUCE

568ml carton single cream
1 vanilla pod
4 large egg yolks
75g (3oz) golden caster sugar
½ level tsp cornflour

TO FINISH

Cocoa powder to dust

This decadent chocolate terrine is smooth, wickedly rich and so tempting. A light, creamy vanilla sauce is the perfect foil.

1 Preheat the oven to 150°C (130°C fan oven) mark 2. Grease and base-line a 900g (2lb) loaf tin.

2 Put the chocolate and cocoa powder in a heatproof bowl over a pan of barely simmering water and leave until melted and glossy, stirring occasionally. Remove the bowl from the pan and allow to cool.

3 Whisk the eggs and muscovado sugar together in a bowl until smooth and creamy. In another bowl, whip the cream until soft peaks form. Gradually fold the melted chocolate and cream into the egg mixture, then incorporate the brandy, if using. Pour into the prepared loaf tin and tap the base on the work surface to level the mixture.

4 Stand the loaf tin in a roasting tray, and fill the tray with hot water to come halfway up the sides. Cover with non-stick baking parchment and bake in the oven for 1¾ hours or until the terrine is just set in the centre. Don't worry if it looks slightly wobbly – the mixture will firm up as it cools. Leave the tin in the tray of water for 30 minutes, then lift out and chill in the fridge overnight.

5 To make the vanilla sauce, put the cream in a heavy-based pan. Split the vanilla pod and scrape the seeds into the cream. Heat gently until the cream just comes to the boil, then set aside to cool and infuse for about 15 minutes.

6 Whisk the egg yolks, sugar and cornflour together in a bowl, add a little of the cooled cream and whisk until smooth. Add the remaining cream and stir well. Pour the sauce back into the rinsed-out pan and stir over a moderate heat for 5 minutes or until thickened enough to lightly coat the back of the spoon. Strain, cool, cover and chill.

7 When ready to serve, dip the loaf tin in a bowl of warm water for 10 seconds, then invert on to a board and shake firmly to unmould. Cut into slices, using a sharp knife dipped into warm water. Lift on to serving plates and pour the vanilla sauce around. Dust with cocoa and serve.

TO PREPARE AHEAD: Prepare the terrine to the end of step 4, and the sauce to the end of step 6. The terrine will keep well in the fridge for up to 4 days, and the sauce for at least 2 days.

LAYERED CHOCOLATE MOUSSE CAKE TERRINE

PREPARATION TIME: 1 hour, plus overnight chilling
COOKING TIME: 45–55 minutes
PER SERVING: 715 cals; 49g fat; 53g carbohydrate

SERVES 6

CAKE LAYER

4 large eggs, separated
125g (4oz) golden caster sugar
25g (1oz) cocoa powder

MOUSSE LAYER

65g (2½oz) unsalted butter
60g (2¼oz) plain, dark chocolate with 70% cocoa solids,
   in pieces
50g (2oz) cocoa powder
284ml carton double cream
25g (1oz) icing sugar
4 large egg yolks
150g (5oz) golden caster sugar

TO FINISH

Single cream to serve
Cocoa powder to dust

Velvety smooth chocolate mousse set between layers of moist, dark chocolate sponge is a chocoholic's idea of heaven. Here there are no other flavours to detract from the smooth richness of chocolate…enjoy!

1 Preheat the oven to 150°C (130°C fan oven) mark 2. To prepare the cake layer, line a 30x23cm (12x9in) Swiss roll tin with non-stick baking parchment.

2 In a bowl, beat the egg yolks with 25g (1oz) of the caster sugar and the cocoa powder. In a clean bowl, whisk the egg whites until stiff, then gradually whisk in the remaining 75g (3oz) sugar to make a stiff, glossy meringue. Beat a quarter of the meringue into the egg yolk mix. Now gently fold this mixture back into the remaining meringue.

3 Pour the cake mixture into the prepared tin and spread out gently into the corners. Bake for 45–55 minutes or until just firm to the touch in the centre. Turn out on to a large sheet of greaseproof paper and carefully peel off the baking parchment. Cool, then cover with a damp cloth.

4 For the mousse, put the butter, chocolate and cocoa into a heatproof bowl and set over a pan of gently simmering water. Leave until melted, stirring occasionally. Remove the bowl from the pan and allow to cool.

5 Whisk the cream with the icing sugar until it begins to thicken. In another bowl, beat the egg yolks with the caster sugar until thick and light in colour, then beat into the cooled chocolate mixture. Slowly whisk in the cream.

6 Line a 1.2 litre (2 pint) loaf tin with non-stick baking parchment. Cut the cake into 3 rectangles, that will fit the tin. Spoon one third of the mousse into the tin and lay a rectangle of cake on top, trimming to fit as necessary. Repeat these layers twice, finishing with cake. Cover the tin with foil and chill in the fridge overnight.

7 When ready to serve, run a knife around the inside of the tin, then invert on to a board and shake firmly to unmould. Cut into thick slices, using a sharp knife dipped into warm water. Lift on to serving plates and drizzle a little single cream around. Dust lightly with cocoa powder and serve.

TO FREEZE: Make the terrine and freeze in the tin. Thaw overnight in the fridge. Turn out and serve as above.

ORANGE AND CHOCOLATE CHEESECAKE

PREPARATION TIME: 45 minutes, plus cooling

COOKING TIME: 2–2¼ hours

PER SERVING (FOR 12): 850 cals; 64g fat;
63g carbohydrate

PER SERVING (FOR 14): 730 cals; 55g fat;
54g carbohydrate

SERVES 12–14

BASE

225g (8oz) chilled butter, plus extra to grease

250g (9oz) plain flour, sifted

150g (5oz) light muscovado sugar

3 level tbsp cocoa powder

TOPPING

2 oranges

4 x 200g tubs cream cheese

250g tub mascarpone

4 large eggs

225g (8oz) golden caster sugar

2 level tbsp cornflour

½ tsp vanilla extract

1 vanilla pod

TO FINISH (OPTIONAL)

Chocolate curls (see page 10)

This luxurious, silky-textured orange and vanilla cheesecake tops a melt-in-the-mouth, thick chocolate biscuit base. It freezes well and is perfect for a special occasion.

1 Preheat the oven to 180°C (160°C fan oven) mark 4. To make the base, grease and base-line a 23cm (9in) spring-release cake tin. Cut 175g (6oz) of the butter into cubes; melt the remaining butter and set aside. Put the flour and cubed butter in a food processor with the sugar and cocoa powder. Whiz together to the texture of fine breadcrumbs, then pour in the melted butter and pulse until the mixture comes together.

2 Spoon into the prepared tin and press with the back of a metal spoon to level the surface. Bake in the oven for 35–40 minutes until lightly puffed; avoid overbrowning otherwise the biscuit base will have a bitter flavour. Remove from the oven; allow to cool. Reduce the oven setting to 150°C (130°C fan oven) mark 2.

3 Meanwhile, make the cheese topping. Grate the zest from the oranges, then squeeze the juice – you will need 150ml (¼ pint). Put the cream cheese, mascarpone, eggs, sugar, cornflour, grated orange zest and vanilla extract into a large bowl. Using an electric hand whisk, beat the ingredients together thoroughly until well combined.

4 Split the vanilla pod in half lengthways, scrape out the seeds, using the tip of a sharp knife, and add them to the cheese mixture. Beat in the orange juice and continue whisking until the mixture is smooth.

5 Pour the cheese mixture over the cooled biscuit base. Bake for about 1½ hours or until pale golden on top, slightly risen and just set around the edge. The cheesecake should still be slightly wobbly in the middle; it will set as it cools. Turn off the oven and leave the cheesecake inside to cool for 1 hour. Remove and allow to cool completely; about 3 hours.

6 Just before serving, unclip the tin and transfer the cheesecake to a plate. Scatter chocolate curls on top to decorate if you like.

TO PREPARE AHEAD: Make the cheesecake to the end of step 5, up to a day ahead. Cover and keep in a cool place. If kept in the fridge, bring the cheesecake back to room temperature before serving. Finish as above.

TO FREEZE: Make the cheesecake to the end of step 5, then wrap and freeze for up to 1 month. To use, thaw at cool room temperature overnight. Complete the recipe as above.

BAKED RICOTTA TORTE

PREPARATION TIME: 20 minutes, plus chilling

COOKING TIME: 40 minutes

PER SERVING: 340 cals; 18g fat; 35g carbohydrate

SERVES 8

125g (4oz) digestive biscuits

50g (2oz) butter

1 lemon

75g (3oz) dark muscovado sugar

250g (9oz) ricotta cheese

300ml (½ pint) natural yogurt

25g (1oz) rice flour, or ground rice

3 large eggs

TO FINISH

Cocoa powder to dust

Chocolate curls (see page 10) to decorate

Ricotta gives this light baked cheesecake a superb velvety texture. For a slimline version – less than 250 calories per slice – use reduced-fat digestives, half-fat butter and low-fat yogurt.

1 Line the base of a 23cm (9in) spring-release cake tin with non-stick baking parchment. Crush the biscuits to a fine powder in a food processor. Melt the butter, add to the processor and pulse until the mixture comes together. Press over the base of the tin and chill for about 30 minutes.

2 Preheat the oven to 180°C (160°C fan oven) mark 4. Grate the zest from the lemon and squeeze the juice – you need 3 tbsp.

3 Put the sugar in the processor and whiz for 1–2 minutes. Add the ricotta and process for 2–3 minutes, then add the lemon zest and juice, yogurt and rice flour. Pulse to mix well, then add the eggs and combine.

4 Pour the cheese mixture over the biscuit base and bake for 40 minutes or until lightly set. Leave to cool in the tin, then chill until ready to serve.

5 To serve, unmould the torte and dust with cocoa powder. Top with chocolate curls to finish.

RASPBERRY AND WHITE CHOCOLATE TARTS

PREPARATION TIME: 40 minutes, plus chilling
COOKING TIME: 40 minutes
PER SERVING: 670 cals; 47g fat; 54g carbohydrate

SERVES 8

PASTRY

225g (8oz) plain flour, plus extra to dust

150g (5oz) butter, cut into cubes

50g (2oz) icing sugar

2–3 drops of vanilla extract

1 large egg, lightly beaten

FILLING

275g (10oz) white chocolate, broken into small pieces

284ml carton double cream

1 vanilla pod, split

2 large eggs, separated

2 tbsp Kirsch

TO FINISH

350–450g (12oz–1lb) raspberries

Icing sugar to dust

These satin-textured white chocolate tarts are generously topped with fresh raspberries and a liberal dusting of icing sugar.

1 To make the pastry, put the flour, cubed butter and icing sugar in a food processor and pulse until the mixture resembles fine crumbs. Add the vanilla extract, and all but 2 tsp of the beaten egg. Pulse until the dough comes together to form a ball. Wrap in clingfilm and chill for at least 30 minutes.

2 Roll out the pastry thinly on a lightly floured surface. Using a saucer as a guide, cut out rounds and use to line eight 9cm (3½in), 3cm (1¼in) deep loose-bottomed tart tins. Don't worry if the pastry cracks as you line the tins – it's easy to patch together. Prick the pastry bases with a fork, then refrigerate for 30 minutes. Preheat the oven to 200°C (180°C fan oven) mark 6.

3 Line the pastry cases with greaseproof paper and baking beans and bake 'blind' for 10 minutes. Remove the paper and beans and return to the oven for 5–10 minutes to cook the bases. Brush with the 2 tsp reserved egg and bake for 1 minute longer to seal; cool slightly. Lower the oven setting to 190°C (170°C fan oven) mark 5.

4 For the filling, put the white chocolate in a bowl. Pour the cream into a small, heavy-based saucepan, add the split vanilla pod and bring just to the boil. Take off the heat and remove the vanilla pod. Slowly pour the hot cream on to the chocolate and stir until the chocolate is completely melted. Cool.

5 Mix the egg yolks and Kirsch into the cooled chocolate mixture. In a clean bowl, whisk the egg whites until they form soft peaks, then fold carefully into the chocolate mixture until evenly incorporated.

6 Pour the filling into the pastry cases and bake for 10–15 minutes until just set. If the filling appears to colour too quickly in the oven, cover with foil. Leave to cool in the tins. Don't worry if the filling seems very soft – it will become firmer on chilling. Refrigerate for at least 5 hours or overnight.

7 Remove the tarts from the fridge 30 minutes before serving. Unmould on to plates and arrange the raspberries on top. Dust generously with icing sugar and serve with chilled pouring cream.

TO FREEZE: Prepare to the end of step 6, then cool, pack and freeze. To use, thaw overnight at cool room temperature and finish as above.

STRAWBERRY CHOCOLATE TART

PREPARATION TIME: 30 minutes, plus chilling
COOKING TIME: 50 minutes
PER SERVING (FOR 6): 900 cals; 62g fat;
66g carbohydrate
PER SERVING (FOR 8): 670 cals; 47g fat;
50g carbohydrate

SERVES 6–8

PASTRY
225g (8oz) plain flour, plus extra to dust
150g (5oz) butter, cut into cubes
50g (2oz) icing sugar
Grated zest of 1 orange
1 large egg, lightly beaten

FILLING
150g (5oz) butter
225g (8oz) plain, dark chocolate with 60–70% cocoa
    solids, finely chopped
3 large eggs, plus 2 yolks
50g (2oz) golden caster sugar
4 tbsp orange liqueur, such as Grand Marnier or
    Cointreau

TOPPING
700g (1½lb) strawberries, halved or quartered
6 level tbsp redcurrant jelly
1 tbsp crème de cassis or orange liqueur, such as
    Grand Marnier or Cointreau

A topping of glazed fresh strawberries perfectly offsets the richness of this delicious, gooey, chocolate mousse tart.

1 To make the pastry, put the flour, butter, icing sugar and grated orange zest in a food processor and whiz until the mixture resembles fine crumbs. Add all but 2 tsp of the beaten egg and pulse until the pastry comes together in a ball. Wrap in clingfilm and chill for 30 minutes.

2 Roll out the pastry on a lightly floured surface and use to line a 23cm (9in), 4cm (1½in) deep, fluted loose-bottomed tart tin. Prick the base and chill for 30 minutes. Preheat the oven to 200°C (180°C fan oven) mark 6.

3 Line the pastry case with greaseproof paper and baking beans and bake 'blind' for 10 minutes. Remove the paper and beans, then bake for a further 10 minutes until the pastry is cooked though. Brush with the reserved egg and return to the oven for 1 minute to seal. Leave to cool slightly. Lower the oven setting to 190°C (170°C fan oven) mark 5.

4 To make the filling, melt the butter in a saucepan. Off the heat, add the chocolate and stir until it is completely melted and smooth. In a large bowl, whisk the eggs, egg yolks and caster sugar together, using an electric whisk, for 5–10 minutes until pale and light. Fold in the melted chocolate mixture and liqueur.

5 Pour the chocolate filling into the pastry case and cook for 15–17 minutes or until the mousse is puffed and has formed a crust on the surface. Remove from the oven and leave to cool in the tin. Don't worry if the chocolate mousse seems runny – it will set as it chills. Refrigerate for 5 hours or overnight.

6 Arrange the strawberries on top of the tart. Warm the redcurrant jelly with the crème de cassis or liqueur until melted and smooth. Brush over the strawberries to glaze. Serve within 4 hours.

VARIATION: Make individual tarts, using six 8cm (3¼in), 3cm (1¼in) deep, loose-bottomed tart tins. Follow the recipe above, reducing the baking time for the filled pastry cases to 10–12 minutes.

ALMOND AND WHITE CHOCOLATE TART

PREPARATION TIME: 1 hour, plus chilling

COOKING TIME: 45–50 minutes

PER SERVING (FOR 6): 830 cals; 48g fat; 94g carbohydrate

PER SERVING (FOR 8): 620 cals; 36g fat; 71g carbohydrate

SERVES 6–8

PASTRY

175g (6oz) plain flour, plus extra to dust

50g (2oz) icing sugar

75g (3oz) butter, cut into cubes

Grated zest of 1 large orange

1 large egg yolk

FILLING

100g (3½oz) white chocolate, broken into small pieces

125g (4oz) butter

125g (4oz) icing sugar

2 large eggs, beaten

125g (4oz) ground almonds

1 level tbsp plain flour

Few drops of vanilla extract

TOPPING

1 small pineapple

1 large orange

Icing sugar to sprinkle

200g (7oz) apricot jam

8 kumquats, sliced (optional)

A wicked white chocolate tart with a lavish, contrasting topping of caramelised pineapple, sliced kumquats and orange segments.

1 To make the pastry, put the flour, icing sugar and butter in a food processor and whiz until the mixture resembles fine breadcrumbs. Add the orange zest, egg yolk and 1–2 tbsp cold water, and pulse until the mixture just comes together. Turn out on to a lightly floured surface and knead lightly, then wrap in clingfilm and chill for 30 minutes.

2 Roll the pastry out thinly on a lightly floured surface and use to line a 23cm (9in), 2.5cm (1in) deep, loose-bottomed tart tin. Chill for 20 minutes. Preheat the oven to 200°C (180°C fan oven) mark 6.

3 Prick the pastry base with a fork, line with greaseproof paper and baking beans and bake 'blind' for 15 minutes. Remove the paper and beans and bake for a further 5 minutes. Turn the oven down to 180°C (160°C fan oven) mark 4. Brush the pastry with a little of the egg for the filling and return to the oven for 1 minute to seal.

4 To make the filling, melt the white chocolate in a bowl over a pan of barely simmering water, stir until smooth and set aside to cool. Put the butter in a large bowl and beat with an electric hand whisk until creamy, then beat in the icing sugar until well combined and fluffy. Gradually beat in the eggs, a little at a time. Add the ground almonds, flour, melted chocolate and vanilla extract; fold in until the mixture is smooth.

5 Pour the filling into the pastry case and smooth the surface. Bake for 25–30 minutes or until just set in the middle. The mixture will puff in the oven and firm up on cooling. Allow to cool for 15 minutes, then carefully put on a wire cooling rack.

6 For the topping, preheat the grill to high. Peel, thinly slice and core the pineapple, then sprinkle the slices heavily with icing sugar and put under the grill until the pineapple is glazed to a light caramel colour; allow to cool. Peel the orange, discarding all white pith, then cut out the segments; set aside.

7 Warm the apricot jam in a small pan over a low heat until melted, then simmer for 1–2 minutes. Sieve and return this glaze to the pan; if it is a little thick, add a splash of water.

8 Arrange the pineapple, orange segments, and kumquats if using, over the top of the tart and brush with a thin layer of the warm jam. Allow the glaze to set before serving.

TO FREEZE: Prepare the tart to the end of stage 5, pack and freeze. To use, thaw at room temperature for 3–4 hours, then continue as above.

CHOCOLATE AND HAZELNUT TART

PREPARATION TIME: 45 minutes, plus chilling
COOKING TIME: 45 minutes
PER SERVING (FOR 8): 650 cals; 46g fat;
53g carbohydrate
PER SERVING (FOR 10): 520 cals; 37g fat;
42g carbohydrate

SERVES 8–10

PASTRY

175g (6oz) plain white flour, plus extra to dust

40g (1½oz) icing sugar

125g (4oz) butter, cut into cubes

1 large egg, lightly beaten

HAZELNUT PASTE

50g (2oz) skinned hazelnuts

25g (1oz) butter

40g (1½oz) stoned dates, preferably fresh, pitted and
    chopped

50ml (2fl oz) golden syrup

1 level tsp plain flour

50g (2oz) light muscovado sugar

1 large egg

CHOCOLATE MOUSSE

150g (5oz) plain, dark chocolate with 70% cocoa solids,
    in pieces

100g (3½oz) unsalted butter, cut into cubes

3 large eggs, separated

50g (2oz) golden caster sugar

GANACHE TOPPING

50g (2oz) plain, dark chocolate with 70% cocoa solids,
    in pieces

15g (½oz) butter

3 tbsp double cream

TO DECORATE

Few strawberries

A rich, decadent chocolate tart is a perfect finale to a special meal. For a glossy finish, carefully wave a blow torch (available from cook's shops) evenly over the surface of the tart before serving.

1 To make the pastry, put the flour, icing sugar and butter in a food processor and whiz until the mixture resembles fine breadcrumbs. Set aside 1 tbsp of the egg. Add the rest to the processor and pulse until the pastry begins to come together, adding 1–2 tsp cold water if necessary. Turn out on to a lightly floured work surface and knead gently until just smooth. Wrap in clingfilm and chill for at least 1 hour.

2 Roll the pastry out very thinly on a lightly floured surface and use to line a 23cm (9in) loose-bottomed tart tin. Refrigerate for 30 minutes. Preheat the oven to 200°C (180°C fan oven) mark 6.

3 Prick the pastry base with a fork, line with greaseproof paper and baking beans and bake 'blind' for 10–15 minutes until just beginning to colour around the edge. Remove the paper and beans and brush the base with the reserved egg to seal. Return to the oven for 2–3 minutes.

4 To make the hazelnut paste, spread the hazelnuts on a baking tray and toast under a preheated grill or in the oven until golden brown. Tip on to a plate, cool, then chop finely. Melt the butter and mix with the chopped nuts and remaining ingredients until evenly blended. Pour into the pastry case and bake for 25–30 minutes or until just set. Leave to cool.

5 To make the mousse, melt the chocolate in a heatproof bowl over a pan of gently simmering water. Stir until smooth, remove from the heat and add the butter, stirring until melted. Beat in the egg yolks. Whisk the egg whites in a clean bowl to soft peaks, then whisk in the caster sugar a spoonful at a time. Continue to whisk until firm. Carefully fold this meringue into the chocolate mixture until evenly combined.

6 Pour the chocolate mousse on to the cooled hazelnut filling, smooth with a spatula, then refrigerate for at least 4 hours or overnight.

7 To prepare the ganache topping, melt the chocolate and butter in a heatproof bowl over a pan of gently simmering water. Stir until smooth and remove from the heat. Add the cream and mix thoroughly.

8 Pour the ganache topping on to the chilled mousse, spreading it evenly to the edges. Allow to set, then mark a decorative criss-cross pattern with a hot knife. Serve in slices, with a few strawberries to the side. Accompany with a dollop of ice cream or crème fraîche if you like.

TO PREPARE AHEAD: Refrigerate the finished tart for up to 2 days.
TO FREEZE: Complete the recipe, then wrap and freeze. To use, thaw the tart overnight at cool room temperature.

CHOCOLATE AND ORANGE TRUFFLE TORTE

PREPARATION TIME: 30 minutes, plus chilling
COOKING TIME: 25–30 minutes
PER SERVING: 560 cals; 44g fat; 30g carbohydrate

SERVES 12

BASE

4 large eggs

125g (4oz) golden caster sugar

40g (1½oz) plain flour

2 level tbsp cocoa powder

20g (¾oz) butter, melted and cooled

4 tbsp orange liqueur, such as Grand Marnier or
    Cointreau

TRUFFLE MIXTURE

450g (1lb) plain, dark chocolate with 70% cocoa solids,
    roughly chopped

568ml carton double cream

4 large egg yolks

50g (2oz) caster sugar

Finely grated zest of 3 large oranges

TO FINISH

Cocoa powder to dust

12 caramelised physalis fruit (see right), optional

Chocolate and orange is a classic partnership that works well in this elegant dessert. We've made the torte large enough for a buffet…or second helpings.

1 Lightly grease a 25cm (10in) loose-bottomed cake tin and base-line with non-stick baking parchment.

2 To make the base, preheat the oven to 180°C (160°C fan oven) mark 4. Using a food mixer, whisk the eggs and sugar together on high speed until the mixture has doubled in volume and is very thick. (Or, beat in a large heatproof bowl over a pan of simmering water, using a hand-held electric whisk, until thick; take off the heat and whisk until cool.)

3 Sift the flour and cocoa together over the mixture and fold in carefully. Drizzle in the melted butter and fold in until just combined; do not over-fold, as this would knock air out of the mixture and result in a flat cake.

4 Pour the mixture into the prepared tin and bake for 25–30 minutes. Leave the cake in the tin for 10 minutes, then turn out on to a wire rack. Drizzle with the orange liqueur and set aside to cool. When cold, return the cake base to the tin, placing it upside down and pressing firmly to fit.

5 For the truffle mixture, put the chocolate in a heatproof bowl with half of the cream and set over a pan of simmering water. Once the chocolate has melted, stir until smooth, remove from the heat and leave to cool.

6 Whisk the remaining cream to soft peaks. In another bowl, beat the egg yolks and sugar together, using an electric whisk, until pale and fluffy. Beat this mixture into the cooled chocolate, then fold into the whipped cream together with the orange zest. Immediately pour the mixture over the cake base in the tin and chill for at least 3 hours until the truffle mixture is set firm, or preferably overnight, before serving.

7 To serve, run a warm knife round the edge of the torte and carefully remove from the tin. Dust with cocoa powder and cut into slices. Decorate with caramelised physalis fruit if you like.

TO PREPARE AHEAD: Refrigerate the torte at stage 6 for up to 2 days.
TO FREEZE AHEAD: Make the torte, then wrap and freeze (without the decoration). To use, thaw the tart overnight at cool room temperature.

CARAMELISED PHYSALIS FRUIT: Fold back the dried petals of the physalis fruit to expose the orange berries; set aside. Dissolve 125g (4oz) golden caster sugar in 75ml (3fl oz) water in a small heavy-based pan over a low heat, then bring to the boil. Bubble until a rich caramel colour, then dip the base of the pan in cold water to stop the cooking process. Immediately dip the physalis berries into the caramel to coat. Put on a lightly oiled baking sheet and leave to set in a dry atmosphere for up to 3 hours.

PROFITEROLES

PREPARATION TIME: 25 minutes, plus cooling
COOKING TIME: 30 minutes
PER SERVING: 660 cals; 54g fat; 38g carbohydrate

SERVES 6

CHOUX PASTE

65g (2½oz) white plain flour
Pinch of salt
50g (2oz) butter, diced
2 large eggs, lightly beaten

CHOCOLATE SAUCE

225g (8oz) plain chocolate, in pieces
142ml carton double cream
1–2 tbsp Grand Marnier to taste (optional)
1–2 tsp golden caster sugar to taste (optional)

TO ASSEMBLE

284ml carton double cream
Few drops of vanilla extract
1 level tsp caster sugar

Universally popular, profiteroles can be made ahead of time and frozen – ideal for parties. Choux pastry isn't difficult, though it can be a little disconcerting the first time you make it. The flour must be added all at once – the mixture will be lumpy at this stage, but it will beat to a smooth and shiny paste. On baking the choux buns puff up to leave a hollow centre. Thorough cooking is essential to ensure that the buns don't collapse.

1 Preheat the oven to 220°C (200°C fan oven) mark 7. Sift the flour with the salt on to a sheet of greaseproof paper. Put the butter in a medium heavy-based saucepan with 150ml (¼ pint) water. Heat gently until the butter melts, then bring to a rapid boil. Take off the heat and immediately tip in all the flour and beat thoroughly with a wooden spoon until the mixture is smooth and forms a ball. Turn into a bowl and leave to cool for about 10 minutes.

2 Gradually add the eggs to the mixture, beating well after each addition. Ensure that the mixture becomes thick and shiny before adding any more egg – if it's added too quickly, the choux paste will become runny and the cooked buns will be flat.

3 Sprinkle a large baking sheet with a little water. Using two damp teaspoons, spoon about 18 small mounds of the choux paste on to the baking sheet, spacing well apart to allow room for them to expand. Alternatively, spoon the choux paste into a piping bag fitted with a 1cm (½in) plain nozzle and pipe mounds on to the baking sheet.

4 Bake for about 25 minutes or until well risen, crisp and golden brown. Make a small hole in the side of each bun to allow the steam to escape and then return to the oven for a further 5 minutes or until thoroughly dried out. Slide on to a large wire rack and set aside to cool.

5 To make the sauce, put the chocolate and cream in a medium saucepan with 4 tbsp water. Heat gently, stirring occasionally, until the chocolate melts to a smooth sauce; do not boil. Remove from the heat.

6 To assemble, lightly whip the cream with the vanilla extract and sugar until it just holds its shape. Pipe into the hole in each choux bun, or split the buns open and spoon in the cream. Refrigerate for up to 2 hours.

7 Just before serving, gently reheat the chocolate sauce. Add Grand Marnier and sugar to taste, if you wish. Divide the choux buns between serving bowls and pour over the warm chocolate sauce. Serve immediately.

TO FREEZE: Bake the choux buns, cool and freeze at the end of stage 4. To use, put the frozen buns on a baking sheet in the oven at 220°C (200°C fan oven) mark 7 for 5 minutes. Cool and complete the recipe.

CHOCOLATE CROQUEMBOUCHE

PREPARATION TIME: 45 minutes, plus standing
COOKING TIME: 25 minutes
PER SERVING: 660 cals; 50g fat; 49g carbohydrate

SERVES 12

CHOUX PASTE

100g (3¼oz) white plain flour

Pinch of salt

1½ level tsp cocoa powder

75g (3oz) butter, diced

3 large eggs, lightly beaten

TO ASSEMBLE

225g (8oz) packet ready-made shortcrust pastry

75g (3oz) unskinned almonds

75g (3oz) granulated sugar

450ml (¾ pint) double cream

Icing sugar to dust

CHOCOLATE FUDGE SAUCE

350g (12oz) plain chocolate, in pieces

200ml (7fl oz) double cream

4 level tbsp light muscovado sugar

This tower of choux buns with its cascading chocolate fudge sauce is our chocolate version of the classic French gâteau. Make sure you assemble the pyramid with a wide base, so it won't collapse.

1 Preheat the oven to 220°C (200°C fan oven) mark 7. Prepare the choux paste as for Profiteroles (see left), sifting the cocoa powder with the flour and using 225ml (8fl oz) water.

2 Continue as in steps 3 and 4 of Profiteroles, making about 40 choux buns – you will need to use two baking sheets. Bake each sheet separately for a little less time, about 20 minutes; return them to the oven to dry out. Lower the oven setting to 190°C (170°C fan oven) mark 5.

3 Roll out the shortcrust pastry to a 22–23cm (8½–9in) round. Transfer to a baking sheet and crimp the edges. Prick lightly and bake for about 20 minutes until golden brown. Cool on a wire rack.

4 Put the almonds and granulated sugar in a medium frying pan. Heat gently until the sugar dissolves. Continue to cook until the sugar caramelises, gently prodding the nuts around the pan to prevent them burning. Pour on to an oiled baking sheet and leave to cool and set. Grind the cooled mixture in a food processor or through a mouli-grater to a coarse praline.

5 Lightly whip the cream in a bowl and fold in the ground praline. Split the choux buns open and fill with the cream.

6 Put the shortcrust pastry round on a large flat serving plate. Carefully pile the choux buns on top to form a pyramid shape. Refrigerate for up to 2 hours until ready to serve.

7 To make the sauce, put the chocolate in a medium saucepan with the cream, sugar and 6 tbsp water. Heat gently, stirring occasionally, until the chocolate melts to a smooth sauce; do not boil. Remove from the heat.

8 To serve, dust the choux bun pyramid with icing sugar and drizzle over some of the warm chocolate fudge sauce; serve the rest separately.

TO FREEZE: Bake the choux buns, cool and freeze (unfilled). To use, put the frozen buns on a baking sheet in the oven at 220°C (200°C fan oven) mark 7 for 5 minutes. Cool and complete the recipe.

CHESTNUT AND CHOCOLATE MACAROON

PREPARATION TIME: 45 minutes, plus chilling
COOKING TIME: 1 hour 20 minutes
PER SERVING: 790 cals; 54g fat; 74g carbohydrate

SERVES 6

MERINGUE

175g (6oz) hazelnuts, skinned
275g (10oz) icing sugar
½ level tsp bicarbonate of soda
4 large egg whites

FILLING

50g (2oz) plain, dark chocolate with 70% cocoa solids, in
    pieces
125g (4oz) chestnut purée
1 tbsp maple syrup
200ml (7fl oz) double cream
225g (8oz) mascarpone

TO FINISH

Chocolate curls (see page 10)
Toasted hazelnuts
Edible gold-coated almonds (optional)
Icing sugar to dust

Utterly irresistible, this nutty meringue gâteau is best made at least 4 hours before serving, as the texture becomes exquisitely gooey on standing. It's an excellent dessert around Christmas time.

1 Preheat the oven to 130°C (120°C fan oven) mark ½. Draw three 20cm (8in) circles on non-stick baking parchment. Turn the paper over and put on separate baking sheets. Preheat the grill and spread the nuts out on a baking sheet. Toast under the hot grill until golden brown, then cool completely. Put in a food processor and pulse for a few seconds until finely ground. Sift the icing sugar and bicarbonate of soda together.

2 Whisk the egg whites in a clean bowl until stiff but not dry. Then, with the electric whisk on high speed, gradually whisk in 50g (2oz) of the icing sugar. Using a large metal spoon, carefully fold in the remaining icing sugar and the ground hazelnuts until just combined.

3 Divide the macaroon meringue between the three circles on the baking sheets. Using a round-bladed knife, smooth the mixture out into even rounds. Bake for 5 minutes, then turn the oven setting down to 125°C (105°C fan oven) mark ¼ and bake for a further 1¼ hours. Transpose the baking sheets during baking to ensure even cooking. Cool on a wire rack, then remove and peel away the baking parchment.

4 Meanwhile, put the chocolate in a heatproof bowl over a pan of gently simmering water and leave until melted. Set aside to cool. In a separate bowl, beat together the chestnut purée and maple syrup until smooth.

5 Whip the cream until it just holds its shape and fold it into the mascarpone. Stir half the mascarpone mixture into the cooled, melted chocolate. Fold the remainder into the chestnut purée.

6 Put a meringue round on a large serving plate. Spread with the chestnut mixture. Put a second meringue round on top and press down firmly. Spread with the chocolate cream. Position the final meringue round on top. Refrigerate for at least 4 hours before serving.

7 When ready to serve, decorate with chocolate curls, hazelnuts, and edible gold-coated almonds if using. Dust with sifted icing sugar and serve with single cream if you like.

COOK'S TIP: If your oven only has two shelves, leave one meringue round at kitchen temperature until there is space in the oven to cook it.

TO PREPARE AHEAD: Prepare and assemble the gâteau to the end of step 6 up to 24 hours in advance. Cover and refrigerate. Finish as above.
TO FREEZE AHEAD: Complete to the end of step 6, wrap and freeze. To use, thaw at cool room temperature overnight, then refrigerate until ready to serve. Finish as above.

HAZELNUT MERINGUE GÂTEAU

PREPARATION TIME: 40 minutes, plus cooling
COOKING TIME: About 1½ hours
PER SERVING: 440 cals; 26g fat; 51g carbohydrate

SERVES 10

MERINGUE

5 large egg whites
250g (9oz) golden caster sugar
½ level tsp ground mixed spice
75g (3oz) white chocolate, chopped
75g (3oz) plain chocolate, chopped
125g (4oz) skinned hazelnuts, toasted and chopped

TO ASSEMBLE

75g (3oz) skinned hazelnuts, toasted
125g (4oz) golden caster sugar
284ml carton double cream
Cocoa powder to dust

Luscious, squidgy layers of chocolate flavoured meringue, sandwiched together with cream and hazelnut praline, and finished with a fine dusting of cocoa.

1 Line two baking sheets with non-stick baking parchment. Draw a 23cm (9in) circle on one sheet, using a plate as a guide. On the other sheet draw an 18cm (7in) circle. Turn each piece of paper over. Preheat the oven to 140°C (fan oven 120°C) mark 1.

2 To make the meringue, whisk the egg whites in a bowl until stiff but not dry. Gradually add the sugar, a tablespoon at a time, whisking well after each addition until the meringue is stiff and very shiny. Whisk in the mixed spice with the last of the sugar. Carefully fold in the white and plain chocolate, together with the chopped toasted hazelnuts.

3 Spoon the meringue on to the marked circles on the baking parchment, then spread neatly into rounds. Bake for about 1½ hours until dry and the undersides are firm when tapped, transposing the baking sheets halfway through to ensure even cooking. Turn the oven off and leave the meringues to cool inside.

4 To assemble, put the hazelnuts and sugar in a small, heavy-based saucepan over a gentle heat until the sugar melts. Continue cooking until the sugar caramelises to a rich golden brown colour, then pour on to an oiled baking sheet. Leave to cool and harden.

5 Put the caramel mixture in a polythene bag and roughly crush with a rolling pin to a coarse praline.

6 Lightly whip the cream, then spread evenly over the large meringue and sprinkle with the praline. Cover with the smaller meringue round and dust the top of the gâteau with cocoa powder to serve.

TO FREEZE AHEAD: Pack and freeze the cooled meringue rounds at the end of stage 3. Make the praline and freeze in a separate airtight container. To use, thaw the meringue rounds in the fridge for about 4 hours. Assemble as above.

STRAWBERRY AND CHOCOLATE PAVLOVA

PREPARATION TIME: 40 minutes
COOKING TIME: 1¼ hours
PER SERVING: 380 cals; 21g fat; 47g carbohydrate

SERVES 8

MERINGUE

4 large egg whites

225g (8oz) golden caster sugar

1 level tbsp cornflour

2 tsp distilled malt vinegar

½ tsp vanilla extract

TOPPING

284ml carton double cream

1 level tbsp icing sugar

450g (1lb) strawberries, hulled and halved

TO DECORATE

Chocolate-dipped strawberries (see page 13)

Chocolate curls (see page 10)

Icing sugar to dust

Soft, billowy meringue, covered with whipped cream and piled high with strawberries makes a sensational summer dessert. For sheer decadence, this Pavlova is topped with chocolate curls and chocolate-dipped strawberries, too.

1 Preheat the oven to 130°C (fan oven 120°C) mark ½. Draw a 23cm (9in) circle on a sheet of non-stick baking parchment. Turn the paper over and put on a baking sheet.

2 To make the meringue, using a free-standing electric mixer (or electric hand-held whisk), whisk the egg whites in a bowl until stiff but not dry. Gradually add the sugar, a tablespoon at a time, whisking well after each addition until the meringue is stiff and very shiny. Carefully fold in the cornflour, vinegar and vanilla extract.

3 Spread the meringue on the baking parchment within the marked circle and make a large, shallow hollow in the centre. Rough up the edges with a palette knife. Bake for 1¼ hours or until crisp on the surface and soft within. Leave to cool slightly, then carefully peel off the paper. Don't worry if the meringue cracks slightly at this stage – this is part of its charm! Set aside on a wire rack to cool completely.

4 Up to an hour before serving, lightly whip the cream with the icing sugar to soft peaks. Pile the cream on to the pavlova and scatter the strawberries on top. Leave in a cool place until ready to serve.

5 To serve, decorate with chocolate-dipped strawberries and chocolate curls. Finish with a dusting of icing sugar.

TO PREPARE AHEAD: Make the Pavlova to the end of step 3, then wrap in foil and store in a cool, dry place for up to 3 days. Assemble 1 hour before serving and finish as above.

CHOCOLATE AND HAZELNUT MERINGUES

PREPARATION TIME: 25 minutes, plus softening
COOKING TIME: 2 hours
PER SERVING: 440 cals; 35g fat; 29g carbohydrate

SERVES 6

MERINGUES

125g (4oz) hazelnuts, toasted

125g (4oz) golden caster sugar

75g (3oz) plain, dark chocolate with 70% cocoa solids, in
    pieces

2 large egg whites

TO SERVE

284ml carton double cream

Strawberries and redcurrants

Chocolate curls (see page 10), optional

Meringues that are crisp on the outside, yet soft in the centre, make a delightful dessert, especially when they are topped with cream and soft fruits. For a winter dessert, you could serve them with caramel-dipped physalis fruit (see page 56) and sliced kumquats.

1 Preheat the oven to 110°C (100°C fan oven) mark ¼. Line two baking sheets with non-stick baking parchment. Put the hazelnuts in a food processor with 3 level tbsp caster sugar and process to a fine powder. Add the chocolate and pulse until roughly chopped.

2 In a large, grease-free bowl, whisk the egg whites until stiff. Gradually whisk in the remaining caster sugar, a spoonful at a time, until the meringue is stiff and shiny. Fold in the nut mixture.

3 Put spoonfuls of the meringue in rough mounds, about 9cm (3in) in diameter, on the baking sheets. Bake for about 45 minutes or until the meringues have dried out just enough to peel off the parchment.

4 Gently push in the base of each meringue to form a deep hollow and return to the oven for 1¼ hours or until crisp and dry. Transfer to a wire rack and allow to cool.

5 Whip the cream until it just holds its shape, then spoon three quarters on to the meringues. Leave in the fridge to soften for up to 2 hours.

6 To serve, put a meringue on each serving plate and top with the remaining cream, fruit, and chocolate curls if using. Serve immediately.

TO PREPARE AHEAD: You can make the meringues (to the end of stage 4) up to 5 days in advance and store them in an airtight container in a cool, dry place. Complete the recipe as above.

CHOCOLATE MERINGUE ROULADE

PREPARATION TIME: 30 minutes, plus cooling

COOKING TIME: 1 hour

PER SERVING (FOR 6): 370 cals; 14g fat; 59g carbohydrate

PER SERVING (FOR 8): 280 cals; 10g fat; 44g carbohydrate

SERVES 6–8

5 large egg whites

175g (6oz) golden caster sugar

1 level tsp cornflour

4 level tbsp half-fat crème fraîche

125g (4oz) chocolate spread

50g (2oz) cooked vacuum-packed chestnuts, roughly chopped (optional)

Icing sugar and cocoa powder to dust

Chocolate curls (see page 10) to decorate

It's hard to believe this delicious pudding has so few calories!

1 Preheat the oven to 110°C (100°C fan oven) mark ¼. Line a 31x22cm (12½x8½in) Swiss roll tin with non-stick baking parchment.

2 Using an electric whisk, whisk the egg whites in a large bowl until frothy, then whisk in the sugar. Stand the bowl over a pan of gently simmering water and whisk at high speed until very thick and shiny, about 4–5 minutes. Off the heat, whisk in the cornflour.

3 Spoon into the prepared tin and level. Bake for 1 hour or until just firm on top. Leave to cool for 1 hour; don't worry if the meringue weeps a little.

4 Beat the crème fraîche into the chocolate spread. Fold in the chopped chestnuts, if using.

5 Turn the meringue out on to a sheet of baking parchment dusted with icing sugar and carefully peel off the lining parchment. Make a shallow cut in the meringue, 2.5cm (1in) in from the edge of a short end. Spread the chocolate mixture over the meringue and roll it up, from the cut end.

6 Dust with icing sugar and cocoa and decorate with chocolate curls. Serve with half-fat crème fraîche.

BLACK FOREST ROULADE

PREPARATION TIME: 35 minutes, plus cooling
COOKING TIME: 20 minutes
PER SERVING: 260 cals; 14g fat; 30g carbohydrate

SERVES 10

125g (4oz) plain, dark chocolate with 70% cocoa solids,
  in pieces
4 large eggs, separated
125g (4oz) golden caster sugar, plus extra to dust

FILLING

142ml carton whipping cream
1 level tsp icing sugar
75ml (3fl oz) Greek-style yogurt
2 x 425g cans morello cherries, drained, pitted and
  halved

TO DECORATE

Cocoa powder and icing sugar to dust

Chocolate and cherries are a classic combination. A whipped cream filling, lightened with Greek yogurt, is the perfect contrast to the rich chocolate sponge.

1 Preheat the oven to 180°C (160°C fan oven) mark 4. Line a 33x23cm (13x9in) Swiss roll tin with non-stick baking parchment.
2 Melt the chocolate in a heatproof bowl over a pan of simmering water. Stir until smooth; leave to cool. Whisk the egg yolks and sugar together in a large bowl until thick and creamy. Whisk in the melted chocolate.
3 In a clean bowl, whisk the egg whites until stiff and shiny. Lightly fold into the chocolate mixture. Pour into the prepared Swiss roll tin and level the surface. Bake for 20 minutes or until firm to the touch.
4 Turn the roulade out on to a sugar-dusted sheet of greaseproof paper and peel off the lining parchment. Cover with a damp cloth and leave to cool for 30 minutes.
5 For the filling, lightly whip the cream with the icing sugar, then fold in the yogurt. Spread over the cold roulade and scatter the cherries on top. Roll up from one of the narrow ends, using the greaseproof paper to help. Chill for 30 minutes.
6 Slice the roulade and serve, dusted with cocoa powder and icing sugar.

CHOCOLATE AND PRUNE ROULADE

PREPARATION TIME: 30 minutes, plus soaking and cooling
COOKING TIME: 25 minutes
PER SERVING: 640 cals; 48g fat; 43g carbohydrate

SERVES 8

ROULADE

175g (6oz) plain, dark chocolate with 70% cocoa solids, in pieces
6 large eggs, separated
175g (6oz) golden caster sugar, plus extra to dust
50g (2oz) walnuts, chopped

FILLING

225g (8oz) ready-to-eat pitted prunes
200ml (7fl oz) hot black tea
50g (2oz) unsalted butter, softened
142ml carton double cream
300g tub mascarpone

TO DECORATE

Icing sugar and cocoa powder to dust

A delicious chocolate and walnut flavoured sponge, rolled around a creamy mascarpone and tea-soaked prune filling.

1 Soak the prunes for the filling in the hot tea for 2 hours. Line a 38x28cm (15x11in) Swiss roll tin with non-stick baking parchment.

2 Preheat the oven to 180°C (160°C fan oven) mark 4. Put the chocolate in a small heatproof bowl with 100ml (4fl oz) water. Melt over a saucepan of gently simmering water, then remove from the heat and leave to cool a little. In a large bowl, beat the egg yolks and sugar together until light and thick, then beat in the melted chocolate and chopped walnuts.

3 In a clean bowl, whisk the egg whites to soft peaks. Beat a large spoonful of the egg white into the chocolate mixture to lighten it, then carefully fold in the rest. Immediately pour the mixture into the prepared Swiss roll tin and gently level the surface. Bake for 25 minutes or until just firm to the touch.

4 Leave to cool in the tin for 15 minutes, then cover with greaseproof paper and a damp tea-towel. Leave for 4–6 hours or overnight (this makes it easier to roll).

5 For the filling, drain the prunes, put in a food processor with the softened butter and process until smooth. In a bowl, whip the cream until stiff, then whisk in the mascarpone.

6 Dust a large sheet of greaseproof paper with caster sugar. Carefully turn the roulade out on to the paper and peel away the lining paper. Trim the long sides to neaten if wished. Spread the prune mixture evenly over the roulade, then spread the cream mixture on top. Using the greaseproof paper to help, roll up from a short end to form a tight roll. Dust with icing sugar and cocoa powder to serve.

TO PREPARE AHEAD: Complete to the end of step 4, then wrap and chill overnight. Assemble and serve as above.

TO FREEZE AHEAD: Prepare the roulade to the end of step 4, then pack and freeze. To use, thaw at cool room temperature overnight. Complete the recipe as above.

SPICY POACHED PEARS WITH CHOCOLATE SAUCE

PREPARATION TIME: 20 minutes, plus cooling
COOKING TIME: 25 minutes
PER SERVING: 600 cals; 40g fat; 60g carbohydrate

SERVES 4

125g (4oz) golden caster sugar
Pared zest of ½ lemon
Juice of 1 lemon
3 cloves
1 level tsp crushed black peppercorns
1 rosemary sprig
4 large firm, ripe dessert pears

CHOCOLATE SAUCE

75g (3oz) plain, dark chocolate with 60–70% cocoa
    solids, in pieces
142ml carton double cream
75g (3oz) unsalted butter, cut into cubes

TO DECORATE

Rosemary sprigs and flowers (optional)

Fresh pears are poached in a fragrant sugar syrup, flavoured with warm spices and fresh rosemary, to produce a perfect balance of flavours. A smooth, dark chocolate sauce is the ideal complement.

1 Pour 900ml (1½ pints) water into a medium saucepan and add the caster sugar, pared lemon zest, lemon juice, cloves, crushed black peppercorns and rosemary sprig. Bring slowly to the boil and simmer for 5 minutes.

2 Peel the pears, leaving them whole, and scoop out the cores from the bases, using the tip of a knife or vegetable peeler. For a decorative effect, lightly score lines from the top to the base of the pears in a spiral fashion, using a canelling knife.

3 Add the pears to the sugar syrup; they should fit quite snugly. Reduce the heat, cover the pan and simmer for about 20 minutes until the pears are tender. Set aside to cool.

4 To make the chocolate sauce, put the chocolate, double cream and butter in a saucepan over a gentle heat until melted, then stir until smooth. Set aside to cool.

5 To serve, pour a pool of chocolate sauce on to each serving plate and put a pear in the centre. Decorate with rosemary if wished.

TO PREPARE AHEAD: Cook the pears and make the chocolate sauce up to 2 days in advance; cover and chill. To use, allow the pears to stand at room temperature for 1 hour before serving. Finish as above.

CHOCOLATE CINNAMON SORBET

PREPARATION TIME: 5 minutes, plus chilling and freezing
COOKING TIME: 15 minutes
PER SERVING: 170 cals; 2g fat; 37g carbohydrate

SERVES 6

200g (7oz) golden granulated sugar
50g (2oz) cocoa powder
Pinch of salt
1 level tsp instant espresso coffee powder
1 cinnamon stick
6 tsp crème de cacao (chocolate liqueur) to serve

Sensational dark chocolate sorbet, with a hint of cinnamon. A drizzle of chocolate liqueur is the perfect finishing touch.

1 Put the sugar, cocoa powder, salt, coffee and cinnamon stick in a large pan with 600ml (1 pint) water. Bring to the boil, stirring until the sugar has completely dissolved. Boil for 5 minutes, then remove from the heat. Leave to cool. Remove the cinnamon stick, then chill.

2 If you have an ice-cream maker, put the mixture into it and churn for about 30 minutes until firm. Otherwise, pour into a freezerproof container and put in the coldest part of the freezer until firmly frozen, then transfer the frozen mixture to a blender or food processor and blend until smooth. Quickly put the mixture back in the container and return to the freezer for at least 1 hour.

3 To serve, scoop the sorbet into individual cups and drizzle 1 tsp chocolate liqueur over each portion. Serve immediately.

CHOCOLATE ICE CREAM

PREPARATION TIME: 20 minutes, plus infusing and freezing
COOKING TIME: 15 minutes
PER SERVING (FOR 4): 630 cals; 54g fat; 29g carbohydrate
PER SERVING (FOR 6): 420 cals; 36g fat; 19g carbohydrate

SERVES 4–6

300ml (½ pint) semi-skimmed milk
1 vanilla pod, split
125g (4oz) plain, dark chocolate with 60–70% cocoa
    solids, in pieces
3 large egg yolks
50–75g (2–3oz) golden caster sugar
300ml (½ pint) double cream

Nothing tastes quite like homemade ice cream and this traditional custard-based recipe is a real treat.

1 Pour the milk into a heavy-based saucepan, add the vanilla pod and chocolate and heat gently until the chocolate has melted. Bring almost to the boil, then take off the heat and leave to infuse for 20 minutes.

2 Whisk the egg yolks and sugar together in a bowl until thick and creamy. Gradually whisk in the hot milk, then strain back into the pan. Cook over a low heat, stirring constantly with a wooden spoon, until the custard has thickened enough to lightly coat the back of the spoon; do not allow to boil or it will curdle. Pour into a chilled bowl and allow to cool.

3 Add the double cream to the cold chocolate custard and whisk until evenly blended.

4 Pour into an ice-cream maker and churn for about 30 minutes until frozen. Alternatively freeze in a shallow container, whisking two or three times during freezing to break down the ice crystals and ensure an even-textured result. Allow to soften at cool room temperature for 20–30 minutes before serving.

TIRAMISU ICE CREAM

PREPARATION TIME: 20 minutes, plus freezing
PER SERVING: 370 cals; 23g fat; 32g carbohydrate

SERVES 6

2 level tsp instant espresso coffee powder
4 tbsp Tia Maria
12–16 Savoiardi or sponge fingers
2 medium eggs, separated
75g (3oz) golden caster sugar
250g tub mascarpone
4 tbsp Marsala
1 tsp vanilla extract
25g (1oz) plain, dark chocolate, grated

Delectable Italian-style iced dessert, with a boozy mascarpone filling between layers of sponge fingers and grated chocolate.

1 Double-line a 900g (2lb) loaf tin with clingfilm. Dissolve the coffee in 4 tbsp boiling water, add the Tia Maria and set aside.
2 Line the base of the loaf tin with half of the sponge fingers, placing them widthways and sugared-side down, trimming them as necessary; set aside.
3 Whisk the egg whites in a clean bowl until stiff. Whisk in the sugar 1 tbsp at a time, and continue to whisk until the mixture holds stiff peaks.
4 Beat together the mascarpone, egg yolks, Marsala and vanilla extract. Mix in a large spoonful of the egg whites, then carefully fold in the rest.
5 Drizzle two thirds of the coffee over the sponge fingers and sprinkle the chocolate over. Spoon the mascarpone mixture into the tin and smooth the surface. Arrange the rest of the sponge fingers widthways on top and drizzle over the remaining coffee mixture. Cover and freeze for 5 hours.
6 To serve, invert on to a large serving plate, then lift off the loaf tin and remove the clingfilm. Cut into slices, using a knife dipped in warm water.

MOCHA ICE CREAM

PREPARATION TIME: 20 minutes, plus cooling and freezing
COOKING TIME: 10–15 minutes
PER SERVING: 510 cals; 46g fat; 21g carbohydrate

SERVES 8

600ml (1 pint) double cream
300ml (½ pint) semi-skimmed milk
6 large egg yolks
50g (2oz) golden caster sugar
150ml (¼ pint) strong espresso coffee, cooled
50g (2oz) plain chocolate chips

SAUCE

75g (3oz) plain chocolate, in pieces
Few drops of vanilla extract

A creamy custard-style ice cream, flavoured with espresso coffee and chocolate chips, and served topped with a chocolate sauce.

1 Heat the cream and milk together in a heavy-based pan just to the boil. Meanwhile, beat the egg yolks and sugar together in a bowl until pale and creamy. Slowly pour on the hot cream mixture, whisking all the time. Return to the pan and heat gently, stirring with a wooden spoon until the custard thickens enough to lightly coat the back of the spoon.
2 Strain the custard into a freezerproof container, stir in the coffee and set aside to cool. When cold, stir in the chocolate chips.
3 Freeze the mixture, beating at hourly intervals until the ice cream is firmly frozen, to break down the ice crystals and ensure an even textured result.
4 About 30 minutes before serving, transfer the ice cream to the fridge to soften, and make the sauce. Put the chocolate, vanilla extract and 60ml (2fl oz) water into a saucepan and heat gently until the chocolate is melted. Bring to the boil and let bubble for a few minutes until thickened; set aside to cool slightly.
5 Scoop the ice cream into serving bowls and pour on the chocolate sauce. Serve at once.

3

EVERYDAY CAKES

VANILLA AND WHITE CHOCOLATE CUP CAKES

CHOCOLATE VICTORIA SANDWICH

CHOCOLATE SWISS ROLL

CHOCOLATE MARBLE CAKE

GLUTEN-FREE CHOCOLATE CAKE

EGG-FREE CHOCOLATE LAYER CAKE

FARMHOUSE CHOCOLATE CAKE

SIMPLE CHOCOLATE CAKE

DEVIL'S FOOD CAKE

THE ULTIMATE CHOCOLATE BROWNIES

GLUTEN-FREE BROWNIES

CHERRY CHOCOLATE FUDGE BROWNIES

CHOCOLATE BANANA MUFFINS

TIFFIN CAKE

CHOCOLATE CRACKLES

WICKED CHOCOLATE SLICES

FRUITY ENERGY BARS

FIGGY FRUIT SLICES

CHOCOLATE FUDGE SHORTBREAD

CHOCOLATE VIENNESE FINGERS

FLORENTINES

CHOCOLATE CHIP COOKIES

WHITE AND DARK CHOCOLATE COOKIES

CHERRY CHIP COOKIES

VANILLA AND WHITE CHOCOLATE CUP CAKES

PREPARATION TIME: 25 minutes, plus cooling
COOKING TIME: 15–20 minutes
PER CAKE: 270 cals; 15g fat; 30g carbohydrate

MAKES 12

125g (4oz) butter, at room temperature
125g (4oz) golden caster sugar
1 vanilla pod
2 medium eggs
125g (4oz) self-raising flour, sifted
1 tbsp vanilla extract

TO DECORATE

1 egg white
6 edible violets
Golden caster sugar to dust
200g (7oz) white chocolate flavoured with vanilla,
    in small pieces

These deep, muffin-style, vanilla cup cakes are a far cry from old-fashioned fairy cakes. As an alternative to the frosted violets, you could simply top each cake with a dried cherry.

1 Preheat the oven to 190°C (170°C fan oven) mark 5. Line a 12-hole muffin tin with paper muffin cases.

2 Put the butter and sugar in a bowl. Split the vanilla pod lengthways and scrape out the seeds, adding them to the bowl. Add the remaining cake ingredients and beat thoroughly, using an electric whisk, until smooth and creamy. (Use a free-standing mixer if you have one.)

3 Spoon the mixture into the muffin cases and bake for 15–20 minutes until pale golden, risen and springy to the touch. Leave in the tin for 2–3 minutes, then transfer to a wire rack to cool.

4 To make the decoration, whisk the egg white in a clean bowl for 30 seconds until frothy. Brush over the violet petals and put on a wire rack. Lightly dust with caster sugar and leave to dry.

5 Put the chocolate in a heatproof bowl over a bowl of barely simmering water and leave until melted. Alternatively, microwave on Medium for 2 minutes or until just melted. Stir the chocolate until smooth and let cool slightly.

6 Spoon the white chocolate on to the cakes. Top each with a sugared flower and leave to set before serving.

CHOCOLATE VICTORIA SANDWICH

PREPARATION TIME: 20 minutes, plus cooling
COOKING TIME: 20 minutes
PER SLICE: 520 cals; 30g fat; 62g carbohydrate

MAKES 8 SLICES

175g (6oz) butter, preferably unsalted, softened, plus extra
   to grease
3 level tbsp cocoa powder
175g (6oz) golden caster sugar
3 medium eggs, beaten
160g (5½oz) self raising flour, sifted

TO ASSEMBLE

Chocolate buttercream (see page 141)
Golden caster sugar to dredge

This traditional favourite English cake keeps well and is a good standby to have in the cake tin. If preferred, sandwich with vanilla rather than chocolate-flavoured buttercream, and sprinkle with grated chocolate to finish.

1 Preheat the oven to 190°C (170°C fan oven) mark 5. Grease two 18cm (7in) sandwich tins and base-line each with a round of non-stick baking parchment. Blend the cocoa powder with 3 tbsp hot water to a smooth paste and allow to cool.

2 Cream the butter and sugar together, using a free-standing mixer or electric hand whisk, until pale and fluffy. Add the cooled cocoa mixture and beat until evenly blended.

3 Add the beaten eggs, a little at a time, beating well after each addition. Fold in half of the flour mixture, using a metal spoon or large spatula, then carefully fold in the rest.

4 Divide the mixture evenly between the tins and level the surface with a palette knife. Bake both cakes on the middle shelf of the oven for about 20 minutes, until well risen, springy to the touch and beginning to shrink away from the sides of the tins. Leave in the tins for 5 minutes, then turn out and cool on a wire rack.

5 When the cakes are cool, sandwich them together with chocolate buttercream and sprinkle the top with caster sugar.

PREPARE AHEAD: This cake will keep well for up to 1 week if stored in an airtight tin in a cool larder.
TO FREEZE: Either freeze the finished cake or the individual layers before assembling. Thaw at cool room temperature.

CHOCOLATE SWISS ROLL

PREPARATION TIME: 25 minutes, plus cooling
COOKING TIME: 10–12 minutes
PER SLICE: 320 cals; 11g fat; 52g carbohydrate

MAKES 8 SLICES

3 large eggs
125g (4oz) golden caster sugar
125g (4oz) plain flour, less 1½ tbsp
1½ level tbsp cocoa powder

TO ASSEMBLE

Golden caster sugar to sprinkle
Chocolate buttercream (see page 141), or whipped
   cream
Icing sugar to dust

This classic Swiss roll has an excellent light texture. As the sponge doesn't contain any fat, it doesn't keep well and is best eaten on the day it is made.

1 Preheat the oven to 200°C (180°C fan oven) mark 6. Line a 33x23cm (13x9in) Swiss roll tin with baking parchment.

2 Put the eggs and sugar in a large heatproof bowl and whisk until well blended, using an electric hand whisk. Stand the bowl over a pan of hot water and whisk until the mixture is light and creamy, and thick enough to leave a trail on the surface when the whisk is lifted.

3 Remove the bowl from the saucepan and continue whisking for a further 5 minutes until the mixture is cool and thick.

4 Sift half the flour and cocoa over the mixture and fold in very lightly, using a large metal spoon or plastic spatula. Sift in the remaining flour and cocoa and gently fold in until evenly incorporated. Lightly and carefully fold in 1 tbsp hot water.

5 Pour into the prepared tin and tilt the tin backwards and forwards to spread the mixture evenly. Bake for 10–12 minutes until well risen and the cake springs back when lightly pressed.

6 Meanwhile, lay a sheet of greaseproof paper on a damp tea-towel. Sprinkle the paper generously with caster sugar.

7 Quickly turn out the cake on to the paper and remove the lining paper. Trim off the crusty edges and cover the sponge with a sheet of greaseproof paper. Roll up the warm cake from a short side, with the covering paper inside. Set aside to cool.

8 When cold, carefully unroll and remove the paper. Spread the sponge with buttercream or whipped cream. Re-roll: make the first turn firmly so that the whole cake will roll evenly and have a good shape when finished, but roll more lightly after this turn. Put seam-side down on a wire rack and dust with icing sugar. Serve cut into slices.

TO FREEZE: Make the Swiss roll (to the end of step 7), wrap and freeze. To use, thaw at cool room temperature overnight, then complete the recipe.

CHOCOLATE MARBLE CAKE

PREPARATION TIME: 20 minutes, plus cooling
COOKING TIME: 45 minutes
PER SLICE: 620 cals; 40g fat; 61g carbohydrate

MAKES 8 SLICES

175g (6oz) unsalted butter, softened
175g (6oz) golden caster sugar
3 medium eggs
125g (4oz) self-raising flour
50g (2oz) ground almonds
1 level tsp baking powder
Finely grated zest of 1 orange
1 tbsp brandy
4 level tbsp cocoa powder, sifted

CHOCOLATE GANACHE

200g (7oz) plain chocolate, in pieces
75g (3oz) butter

TO DECORATE

50g (2oz) golden granulated sugar
Juice of 1 orange
8 small kumquats

An impressive marble cake looks professional, yet it is easier to make than you'd imagine. To create the marbled effect, you simply drag a skewer through the two contrasting cake mixtures. A covering of rich chocolate ganache, topped with poached kumquats, is the perfect finish.

1 Preheat the oven to 190°C (170°C fan oven) mark 5. Line a 900g (2lb) loaf tin with a loaf tin liner (or non-stick baking parchment).

2 To make the cake, cream the butter and sugar together in a bowl until pale and light. Beat in the eggs, one at a time.

3 Sift the flour, ground almonds and baking powder together into the bowl and fold in carefully, using a large metal spoon or plastic spatula. Fold in the grated orange zest and brandy. Put half the mixture into another bowl and mix in the cocoa powder.

4 Spoon a dollop of each cake mixture into the prepared tin. Repeat with alternate spoonfuls of the mixtures to create layers. Shake the tin once, then drag a skewer through the mixture to create a marbled effect. Bake for 45 minutes or until a skewer inserted in the centre comes out clean. Turn the cake out on to a wire rack and leave to cool.

5 To finish, melt the chocolate and butter in a heatproof bowl over a pan of hot water; stir the ganache until smooth. Take the cake out of the liner, return to the wire rack and position over a tray. Pour the chocolate ganache over the cake to completely cover it, and leave to set in a cool place for 30 minutes.

6 Put the granulated sugar in a pan. Strain the orange juice into a jug and add enough water to make up to 150ml (¼ pint). Pour on to the sugar and heat gently to dissolve. Add the kumquats and poach for 5–10 minutes. Remove from the heat and set aside to cool.

7 Arrange the cooled, poached kumquats on top of the cake and cut into slices to serve.

TO FREEZE: Make the marble cake (to the end of step 4), wrap and freeze. To use, thaw at cool room temperature overnight, then complete the recipe as above.

GLUTEN-FREE CHOCOLATE CAKE

PREPARATION TIME: 40 minutes, plus cooling
COOKING TIME: 45 minutes–1 hour
PER SLICE: 620 cals; 38g fat; 66g carbohydrate

MAKES 10 SLICES

125g (4oz) butter, softened, plus extra to grease

125g (4oz) gluten-free plain chocolate, in pieces

200g (7oz) light muscovado sugar

2 large eggs, lightly beaten

100ml (3½fl oz) natural yogurt

Few drops of vanilla extract

200g (7oz) brown rice flour

½ level tsp wheat-free baking powder

1 level tsp bicarbonate of soda

ICING

300g (11oz) gluten-free plain chocolate, in pieces

284ml carton double cream

There is no need to deprive yourself of chocolate cake if you are on a gluten- or wheat-free diet. Readily available Bournville plain chocolate is gluten-free.

1 Preheat the oven to 180°C (160°C fan oven) mark 4. Grease and base-line an 18cm (7in) round, deep cake tin with greaseproof paper.

2 Put the chocolate in a heatproof bowl over a pan of simmering water and leave until melted. Stir until smooth and allow to cool slightly.

3 Cream the butter and sugar together until light and fluffy. Gradually beat in the eggs, then the melted chocolate, yogurt and vanilla extract.

4 Sift together the flour, baking powder and bicarbonate of soda. Beat into the cake mixture a little at a time.

5 Turn the mixture into the prepared tin and bake for 45 minutes–1 hour or until a skewer inserted in the centre comes out clean. Leave to cool in the tin for 10 minutes, then transfer to a wire rack to cool completely.

6 To make the icing, put the chocolate in a heatproof bowl. Heat the cream to boiling point and pour on to the chocolate. Leave for 5 minutes, then beat until the chocolate has melted and the mixture is smooth. Allow to cool until thickened, then spread over the cake with a palette knife.

EGG-FREE CHOCOLATE LAYER CAKE

PREPARATION TIME: 40 minutes, plus cooling
COOKING TIME: 1–1¼ hours
PER SLICE: 580 cals; 34g fat; 65g carbohydrate

MAKES 12 SLICES

150ml (¼ pint) sunflower oil, plus extra to grease
75g (3oz) creamed coconut
25g (1oz) plain chocolate, in pieces
50g (2oz) cocoa powder
350g (12oz) self-raising flour
1 level tsp baking powder
Pinch of salt
175g (6oz) light muscovado sugar

ICING

142ml carton double cream
350g (12oz) plain chocolate, in small pieces

Finding suitable cake recipes to bake if you are cooking for someone on an egg-free diet isn't easy, but this recipe is moistened with creamed coconut and sunflower oil rather than eggs...and it's delicious.

1 Preheat the oven to 180°C (160°C fan oven) mark 4. Grease and line a 1.7 litre (3 pint) loaf tin.
2 Put the creamed coconut in a bowl, pour on 425ml (17fl oz) boiling water and stir to dissolve. Set aside to cool for 30 minutes.
3 Melt the chocolate in a heatproof bowl over a pan of simmering water. Stir until smooth and let cool slightly.
4 Sift the cocoa, flour, baking powder and salt together into a bowl. Stir in the sugar and make a well in the middle. Add the coconut mixture, melted chocolate and sunflower oil. Beat to make a smooth batter.
5 Pour the cake batter into the tin. Bake for 1–1¼ hours or until risen and just firm to touch, covering with foil after about 40 minutes. Leave in the tin for 10 minutes, then transfer to a wire rack to cool.
6 To make the icing, pour the cream into a saucepan and bring to the boil. Remove from the heat, add the chocolate and stir until melted. Allow to cool, beating occasionally, until thick.
7 Cut the cake in half horizontally and sandwich the layers together with half of the icing. Spread the rest evenly over the top and sides of the cake. This cake will keep for 2 to 3 days in an airtight tin.

FARMHOUSE CHOCOLATE CAKE

PREPARATION TIME: 20 minutes, plus cooling
COOKING TIME: About 1 hour
PER SLICE: 440 cals; 24g fat; 54g carbohydrate

MAKES 8 SLICES

100g (4oz) butter, in pieces, plus extra to grease
175g (6oz) self-raising flour
Pinch of salt
3 level tbsp cocoa powder
100g (4oz) golden caster sugar
50g (2oz) desiccated coconut
1 egg, beaten
½ tsp vanilla extract
6–8 tbsp semi-skimmed milk to mix
Chocolate buttercream (see page 141), to fill
Icing sugar to dust

This everyday family cake is made by the traditional rubbing-in method. It is important to add the right amount of liquid to achieve the correct consistency: too much will give a heavy texture; too little will result in a dry cake. The mixture should drop easily from the spoon when it is lightly tapped against the side of the bowl.

1 Preheat the oven to 170°C (150°C fan oven) mark 3. Grease and line a 15cm (6in) round, deep cake tin.
2 Sift the flour, salt and cocoa powder together into a bowl. Add the butter and rub into the flour, using your fingertips, until the mixture resembles fine breadcrumbs. Stir in the sugar and desiccated coconut.
3 Make a well in the centre and pour in the egg, vanilla and 6 tbsp milk. Gradually beat into the dry ingredients until the mixture is smooth and has a soft, dropping consistency, adding a little more milk if necessary.
4 Spoon into the cake tin and gently level the surface. Bake for about 1 hour, until well risen and firm to the touch. Turn out and cool on a wire rack.
5 Split the cake into two layers and sandwich together with chocolate buttercream. Dust with icing sugar to serve.

SIMPLE CHOCOLATE CAKE

PREPARATION TIME: 20 minutes, plus cooling
COOKING TIME: 1–1¼ hours
PER SERVING: 540 cals; 24g fat; 81g carbohydrate

MAKES 8 SLICES

100g (4oz) butter, softened, plus extra to grease
100g (4oz) plain chocolate, in pieces
75g (3oz) self-raising flour
2 level tbsp ground rice
75g (3oz) golden caster sugar
1–2 tsp vanilla extract
2 large eggs, beaten

TO ASSEMBLE

Chocolate buttercream (see page 141)
Chocolate glacé icing (see page 141)
Crystallised violets or chocolate buttons

Popular with children and adults alike, this teatime classic is filled with buttercream and topped with glacé icing. For a less rich cake, omit the glacé icing and simply dust the top with icing sugar.

1 Preheat the oven to 180°C (160°C fan oven) mark 4. Grease and line a 15cm (6in) round, deep cake tin.
2 Melt the chocolate in a heatproof bowl over a pan of hot water; stir until smooth and cool slightly. Mix the flour with the ground rice; set aside.
3 Cream the butter, sugar and vanilla extract together in a bowl until pale and fluffy. Add the melted chocolate (which should be only just warm) and mix together lightly. Beat in the eggs, a little at a time. Fold in the flour mixture, using a large metal spoon.
4 Turn the mixture into the prepared tin and bake for 1–1¼ hours until a skewer inserted in the centre comes out clean. Turn out and cool on a wire rack.
5 When cold, split in half and fill with buttercream. Cover the top with glacé icing and leave until almost set before decorating with crystallised violets or chocolate buttons.

DEVIL'S FOOD CAKE

PREPARATION TIME: 40 minutes, plus cooling
COOKING TIME: 40 minutes
PER SLICE: 790 cals; 30g fat; 132g carbohydrate

MAKES 10 SLICES

75g (3oz) butter, softened, plus extra to grease
275g (10oz) plain flour
2 level tsp bicarbonate of soda
½ level tsp salt
100g (4oz) plain chocolate, in pieces
250g (9oz) light muscovado sugar
2 large eggs, lightly beaten
200ml (7fl oz) semi-skimmed milk
1 tsp vanilla extract

FILLING

75g (3oz) butter, softened
Few drops of vanilla extract
175g (6oz) icing sugar
1 tsp semi-skimmed milk

FROSTING

175g (6oz) chocolate dots
450g (1lb) icing sugar, sifted
2 egg yolks
75g (3oz) butter, melted

This rich chocolate layer cake, filled with vanilla buttercream and swirled generously with chocolate frosting, originates from the United States.

1 Preheat the oven to 180°C (160°C fan oven) mark 4. Grease and line two 22cm (8½in) sandwich tins, extending the lining paper above the rims.

2 Sift together the flour, bicarbonate of soda and salt; set aside. Melt the chocolate in a heatproof bowl over a pan of simmering water; stir until smooth and cool slightly.

3 Cream the butter and sugar together in a bowl until pale and fluffy, then gradually add the eggs, beating well after each addition. Slowly add the melted chocolate and beat until well combined. Then carefully fold in the flour mixture, alternately with the milk and vanilla extract, using a large metal spoon.

4 Turn the mixture into the prepared tins and bake for about 40 minutes until the cakes spring back when lightly pressed. Turn out and cool on a wire rack.

5 To make the filling, beat the butter with the vanilla extract until very soft, then gradually beat in the sifted icing sugar with the milk. Sandwich the cakes together with the filling.

6 To make the frosting, melt the chocolate dots in a bowl over a pan of barely simmering water. Take off the heat and stir in the sifted icing sugar and 2 tbsp hot water. Gradually beat in the egg yolks, one at a time, followed by the melted butter, a little at a time. Continue to beat until the frosting is a spreadable consistency.

7 Spread the frosting over the top and sides of the cake, using a palette knife, and mark decoratively in swirls. Leave to set in a cool place (but not the fridge) until set, preferably until the next day, before slicing.

THE ULTIMATE CHOCOLATE BROWNIES

PREPARATION TIME: 20 minutes, plus cooling
COOKING TIME: 1¼ hours
PER BROWNIE: 380 cals; 28g fat; 25g carbohydrate

MAKES 16

200g (7oz) salted butter, plus extra to grease
400g (14oz) plain, dark chocolate with 70% cocoa solids,
    in pieces
225g (8oz) light muscovado sugar
1 tsp vanilla extract
150g (5oz) pecan nuts, roughly chopped
25g (1oz) cocoa powder, sifted
75g (3oz) self-raising flour, sifted
3 large eggs, beaten
Cocoa powder, sifted, to dust

Serve these squidgy, pecan-rich brownies as a teatime treat, with coffee, or as a dessert with ice cream or crème fraîche.

1 Preheat the oven to 170°C (150°C fan oven) mark 3. Grease and baseline a 20cm (8in) square baking tin, 5cm (2in) deep, with non-stick baking parchment.

2 Melt the chocolate with the butter in a heatproof bowl over a pan of gently simmering water; stir until smooth. Remove from the heat and leave to cool slightly. Stir in the sugar, vanilla extract, chopped pecans, cocoa, flour and eggs.

3 Turn the mixture into the prepared tin and level with the back of a spoon. Bake for about 1¼ hours until set to the centre on the surface but still soft underneath. Do not overcook or the soft, gooey texture will be spoilt. Leave to cool in the tin for 2 hours.

4 Turn the cake out on to a board and trim the edges. Dust with sifted cocoa and cut into squares. Serve cold, or slightly warm with ice cream.

TO FREEZE: Bake the brownies, cool, wrap and freeze. To use, unwrap and leave to thaw at cool room temperature for 2–3 hours.

GLUTEN-FREE BROWNIES

PREPARATION TIME: 25 minutes, plus cooling
COOKING TIME: 55 minutes
PER BROWNIE: 410 cals; 29g fat; 35g carbohydrate

MAKES 9

150g (5oz) butter, softened, plus extra to grease
150g (5oz) gluten-free plain chocolate
1½ level tsp instant coffee granules
150g (5oz) golden caster sugar
3 eggs, separated
60g (2½oz) ground almonds
75g (3oz) walnuts, roughly chopped
60g (2½oz) cornflour

You can still enjoy gooey brownies on a gluten- or wheat-free diet. Make sure you buy gluten-free chocolate, such as Bournville. Store the brownies in an airtight tin for 2–3 days, or freeze (as above).

1 Preheat the oven to 180°C (160°C fan oven) mark 4. Grease and line an 18cm (7in) square baking tin, 5cm (2in) deep, with non-stick baking parchment.

2 Melt the chocolate with the coffee granules in a heatproof bowl over a pan of simmering water. Leave to cool slightly.

3 Cream the butter and sugar together in a bowl until light and fluffy, then beat in the egg yolks, one at a time. Fold in the ground almonds, walnuts, cornflour and melted chocolate mixture. In a clean bowl, whisk the egg whites to soft peaks, then gently fold into the mixture.

4 Pour the mixture into the prepared tin. Bake for about 55 minutes until a skewer inserted into the centre comes out clean, covering with grease-proof paper after about 30 minutes. Leave in the tin for 10 minutes, then transfer to a wire rack to cool. Cut into squares to serve.

CHERRY CHOCOLATE FUDGE BROWNIES

PREPARATION TIME: 20 minutes, plus cooling
COOKING TIME: 50 minutes
PER BROWNIE: 460 cals; 27g fat; 46g carbohydrate

MAKES 12

150g (5oz) unsalted butter, plus extra to grease
200g (7oz) plain, dark chocolate with 70% cocoa solids, in pieces
175g (6oz) golden caster sugar
2 tsp vanilla extract
5 medium eggs
175g (6oz) plain flour
¾ level tsp baking powder
250g (9oz) natural glacé cherries, halved

ICING

150g (5oz) plain, dark chocolate with 70% cocoa solids, in pieces
2 tbsp Kirsch
4 tbsp double cream

TO FINISH

Icing sugar and cocoa powder, sifted together, to dust

Irresistible, fudgey brownies flavoured with natural glacé cherries and topped with a Kirsch-flavoured chocolate ganache. Serve as a dreamy dessert with cream, or as a teatime treat.

1 Preheat the oven to 180°C (160°C fan oven) mark 4. Grease and base-line an 18cm (7in) square cake tin, 5cm (2in) deep. Put the butter and chocolate in a bowl over a pan of simmering water and leave until melted. Remove from the heat and stir until smooth. Allow to cool.

2 Whisk the sugar, vanilla extract and eggs together in a bowl until thick, pale and frothy. Stir in the melted chocolate mixture.

3 Sift the flour and baking powder together over the mixture and fold in lightly, together with the glacé cherries. Pour the mixture into the prepared tin.

4 Bake for 50 minutes or until just set and firm to the touch on the surface in the centre, but still soft underneath. If it appears to be overbrowning in the oven, cover with greaseproof paper after about 30 minutes. Leave to cool for about 10 minutes in the tin, then turn out on to a wire rack to cool completely.

5 To make the icing, put the chocolate and Kirsch in a heatproof bowl over a pan of simmering water. Once melted, add the cream mixed with 4 tbsp water, and stir well. Pour the icing over the brownie and leave until set.

6 Cut the brownie into slices and dust with icing sugar sifted with cocoa. Serve with lightly whipped double cream.

TO PREPARE AHEAD: Complete the recipe to the end of step 5, put in an airtight tin and leave in a cool place for up to a day in advance. To use, cut into slices and finish as above.

TO FREEZE: Prepare the brownie to the end of step 4, wrap and freeze. To use, thaw at cool room temperature for about 5 hours. Complete the recipe as above.

CHOCOLATE BANANA MUFFINS

PREPARATION TIME: 15 minutes, plus cooling

COOKING TIME: 20 minutes

PER MUFFIN: 210 cals; 7g fat; 36g carbohydrate

MAKES 12

275g (10oz) self-raising flour

1 level tsp bicarbonate of soda

½ level tsp salt

3 large bananas, about 450g (1lb) in total

125g (4oz) golden caster sugar

1 large egg, beaten

50ml (2fl oz) semi-skimmed milk

75g (3oz) butter, melted and cooled

50g (2oz) plain chocolate, chopped

Home-baked muffins have a wonderful melt-in-the-mouth, crumbly texture, and this recipe is a great way to use up over-ripe bananas. The muffins are best eaten warm soon after they've come out of the oven. Serve with tea or coffee, or with a scoop of vanilla ice cream for a heavenly pudding.

1 Preheat the oven to 180°C (160°C fan oven) mark 4. Line a muffin tray with 12 muffin paper cases. Sift the flour, bicarbonate of soda and salt together into a large mixing bowl and put to one side.

2 Peel the bananas and mash with a fork in a bowl. Add the caster sugar, egg, milk and melted butter, and mix until well combined.

3 Add this to the flour mixture, together with the chopped chocolate. Stir gently, using only a few strokes, until the flour is only just incorporated; do not over-mix. The mixture will be lumpy and rather like batter in consistency.

4 Spoon the mixture into the muffin cases, half-filling them. Bake in the oven for 20 minutes or until the muffins are well risen and golden. Transfer to a wire rack to cool. Serve warm or cold.

TO FREEZE: Bake the muffins and allow to cool. Once cold, pack and freeze in a sealed bag. To use, thaw the muffins individually in the microwave, as needed, allowing 30 seconds on high.

VARIATION: Sprinkle 25g (1oz) roasted and roughly chopped pecan nuts on top of the muffins before baking.

TIFFIN CAKE

PREPARATION TIME: 40 minutes, plus cooling
and overnight chilling
PER WEDGE: 570 cals; 36g fat; 54g carbohydrate

MAKES 8 WEDGES

125g (4oz) butter, plus extra to grease
50g (2oz) raisins
75g (3oz) pitted dates, chopped
4 tbsp brandy
200g (7oz) plain chocolate, in pieces
3 tbsp golden syrup
250g (9oz) digestive biscuits, roughly crushed
Grated zest of ½ large orange

TOPPING
150g (5oz) plain, dark chocolate with 70% cocoa solids,
    in pieces
25g (1oz) butter

This tempting 'refrigerator cake' combines chocolate with dried
fruit, orange zest and crushed biscuits, and is spiked with brandy.
You can store it in the fridge for up to a week. It makes a delightful
edible gift, packed into boxes.

1 Lightly grease and base-line a 20cm (8in) round cake tin, about 4cm
   (1½in) deep.
2 Put the raisins and dates in a bowl. Pour on the brandy and leave the
   dried fruit to soak for 30 minutes.
3 Melt the chocolate with the butter and golden syrup in a heavy-based
   pan over a gentle heat. Remove from the heat.
4 Add the crushed biscuits, orange zest, raisins and dates, together with
   any remaining brandy. Mix well, pour into the prepared tin and spread
   evenly. Allow to cool, then chill for 1 hour.
5 For the topping, melt the chocolate with the butter in a heatproof bowl
   over a pan of simmering water. Stir until smooth, cool, then pour over
   the biscuit layer. Chill in the fridge overnight. Cut into wedges to serve.

TO FREEZE: Make the tiffin, to the end of step 4, then wrap and freeze for
up to 2 months. Thaw at cool room temperature for 4 hours. Complete
the recipe as above.

CHOCOLATE CRACKLES

PREPARATION TIME: 10 minutes, plus chilling
PER CRACKLE: 150 cals; 9g fat; 17g carbohydrate

MAKES 12

225g (8oz) plain or milk chocolate, in pieces
1 tbsp golden syrup
50g (2oz) butter or margarine
50g (2oz) Corn Flakes or Rice Krispies

Children adore these crunchy, no-bake chocolate treats and they
are simple enough for keen young cooks to make themselves.
Keep a supply in the cake tin for teatime, or lunch box treats.

1 Put 12 paper cake cases in a bun tin tray.
2 Put the chocolate, syrup and butter in a heavy-based saucepan over a low
   heat until melted; stir until smooth.
3 Fold in the cereal until evenly mixed, then divide the mixture evenly
   between the paper cases. Chill in the refrigerator until set.

WICKED CHOCOLATE SLICES

PREPARATION TIME: 10 minutes, plus cooling
and chilling
PER SLICE: 270 cals; 19g fat; 25g carbohydrate

MAKES 20

225g (8oz) butter (or Olivio), plus extra to grease
3 tbsp golden syrup
50g (2oz) cocoa powder, sifted
300g packet digestive biscuits, roughly crushed
400g (14oz) plain chocolate, in pieces

Scrumptious, crunchy chocolate morsels that are quick and easy to make – and don't even need to be baked. Children and adults alike will find them incredibly more-ish and they won't last long in your cake tin!

1 Grease a 26x16cm (10x6½in) shallow rectangular cake tin. Put the butter (or Olivio), golden syrup and cocoa powder in a bowl. Melt in the microwave on High, allowing 20 seconds in a 900W model. (Alternatively, melt in a heavy-based pan on a very low heat, then remove from the heat). Stir well until evenly combined.

2 Add the crushed digestive biscuits and mix thoroughly until the biscuit pieces are well coated in the cocoa mixture, crushing down any larger pieces as you do so.

3 Spoon the mixture into the prepared tin. Allow to cool, then cover and chill for 30 minutes.

4 Put the chocolate in a bowl and melt in the microwave on High, allowing 1 minute 40 seconds in a 900W model. Alternatively, melt in a heatproof bowl over a pan of simmering water. Stir once until smooth and let cool slightly.

5 Pour the melted chocolate over the biscuit base, then put the tin in the fridge for 30 minutes or until the topping has set.

6 Using a sharp knife, cut the rectangle in half lengthways in the tin, then cut each section into 10 slices.

FRUITY ENERGY BARS

PREPARATION TIME: 10 minutes, plus standing
PER BAR: 180 cals; 9g fat; 21g carbohydrate

MAKES 12

250g packet ready-to-eat dried apricots
250g packet ready-to-eat dried papaya
50g (2oz) ready-to-eat dried mango
50g (2oz) plain chocolate, chopped
50g (2oz) pecan nuts, chopped and toasted
50g (2oz) brazil nuts, chopped and toasted
1 level tbsp pumpkin seeds
1 level tbsp sesame seeds
1 level tbsp sunflower seeds
¼ level tsp ground nutmeg
2 tbsp Malibu (coconut liqueur)

These little healthy treats are ideal energy boosters as they are packed with nutrients: calcium from the dried fruits; antioxidants from the papaya and brazil nuts; vitamin E and polyunsaturates from the seeds. You will need rice paper to line the baking tin and wrap the bars.

1 Line a 23x18cm (9x7in) shallow baking tin with rice paper. Put the dried apricots, papaya and mango in a food processor and whiz for 15 seconds to mince the fruit. Tip into a bowl.
2 Add the chopped chocolate, nuts, seeds, nutmeg and Malibu to the bowl. Mix everything together well, using your hands.
3 Turn the mixture into the prepared tin, spread level and press to flatten with the back of a spoon. Leave to firm up, then cut into 12 bars and wrap each one in rice paper.

FIGGY FRUIT SLICES

PREPARATION TIME: 30 minutes, plus chilling
COOKING TIME: 10 minutes
PER SLICE: 560 cals; 17g fat; 89g carbohydrate

MAKES 4

2 x 250g packs ready-to-eat dried figs, hard stalks
    removed
50g (2oz) candied orange peel, finely chopped
75g (3oz) hazelnuts, toasted
50g (2oz) shelled pistachio nuts
50g (2oz) plain chocolate
50g (2oz) ready-to-eat pitted dates
¼ level tsp ground cinnamon
Pinch of ground nutmeg
4 tbsp brandy, plus extra to drizzle

Fruity treats to serve after dinner with coffee, or to wrap and take out as a picnic snack. Buy large pieces of candied orange peel for this – usually sold in a box together with pieces of candied lemon and lime peel – rather than the kind that comes ready-chopped. You will also need some rice paper.

1 Put the figs and candied orange peel in a food processor and whiz for 1 minute to mince the fruit finely. Tip into a large bowl.
2 Put the toasted hazelnuts, pistachio nuts, chocolate and dates in the food processor with the spices and 4 tbsp brandy, and pulse to chop roughly. Add to the fig mixture and mix together using your hands.
3 Put a sheet of rice paper on a baking tray. Spoon the fig mixture evenly on top, then press down with the back of a wet spoon to form an even layer. Put another sheet of rice paper on top and press down well. Chill for 1 hour.
4 Cut into 4 rectangles to serve. If not serving straightaway, wrap in non-stick baking parchment and tie up with string. Store in the fridge for up to 4 weeks, unwrapping and drizzling with 1 tsp brandy every week.

COOK'S TIP: If the orange peel is hard, put it in a small pan of cold water, bring to the boil, and simmer for 5 minutes before using.

CHOCOLATE FUDGE SHORTBREAD

PREPARATION TIME: 30 minutes, plus cooling
COOKING TIME: 20 minutes
PER SQUARE: 350 cals; 15g fat; 50g carbohydrate

MAKES 20 SQUARES

175g (6oz) butter, at room temperature, diced, plus
   extra to grease
250g (9oz) plain flour
75g (3oz) golden caster sugar

TOPPING
2 x 397g cans sweetened condensed milk
90g (3½oz) light muscovado sugar
90g (3½oz) butter
250g (9oz) plain chocolate, in pieces

Shortbread topped with fudge and chocolate...pure indulgence.

1 Preheat the oven to 180°C (160°C fan oven) mark 4. Grease and line a 30x22cm (12x8½in) Swiss roll tin.

2 Put the flour, caster sugar and butter in a food processor and blend until the mixture forms crumbs, then pulse a little more until it forms a ball. Turn out on to a lightly floured surface and knead lightly to combine.

3 Press the mixture into the prepared tin and bake for 20 minutes until firm to the touch and very pale brown.

4 For the caramel, put the condensed milk, sugar and butter into a bowl and microwave on High for 12 minutes until the mixture is thick and fudgey, beating with a balloon whisk every 2–3 minutes. (Or put the ingredients in a non-stick pan and cook over a moderate heat, stirring continuously.) Spoon the caramel on to the shortbread, smooth over and allow to cool.

5 To finish, melt the chocolate in a bowl in the microwave on Medium for 2 minutes (or over simmering water), then pour over the caramel layer. Leave to set at room temperature, then cut into squares to serve.

CHOCOLATE VIENNESE FINGERS

PREPARATION TIME: 30 minutes, plus cooling
COOKING TIME: 15–20 minutes
PER FINGER: 100 cals; 6g fat; 9g carbohydrate

MAKES ABOUT 20

25g (1oz) plain chocolate, in pieces
125g (4oz) butter, softened
25g (1oz) icing sugar, sifted
125g (4oz) plain flour
¼ level tsp baking powder
1 tbsp drinking chocolate powder
Few drops of vanilla extract

TO FINISH
50g (2oz) plain chocolate, in pieces

Melt-in-the-mouth chocolate shortbread fingers, dipped in melted chocolate for a decorative finish, are the perfect teatime treat.

1 Preheat the oven to 180°C (160°C fan oven) mark 4. Melt the chocolate in a bowl over a pan of simmering water; stir until smooth and cool slightly.
2 Beat the butter until creamy, then beat in the icing sugar until the mixture is light and fluffy. Beat in the chocolate. Sift in the flour, baking powder and chocolate powder. Beat well, adding the vanilla extract.
3 Put the mixture into a piping bag fitted with a medium star nozzle. Pipe finger shapes, about 7.5cm (3in) long, on to two greased baking sheets, spacing them well apart to allow for spreading. Bake for 15–20 minutes.
4 Leave on the baking sheet for a few minutes, then transfer to a wire rack to cool completely.
5 Melt the chocolate in a bowl over a pan of simmering water; stir until smooth. Dip both ends of each shortbread finger into the chocolate to coat and put on the wire rack. Leave until set before serving.

FLORENTINES

PREPARATION TIME: 15 minutes, plus cooling
COOKING TIME: 8–10 minutes
PER BISCUIT: 110 cals; 7g fat; 11g carbohydrate

MAKES 18

60g (2½oz) unsalted butter
50g (2oz) golden caster sugar
2 tbsp double cream
25g (1oz) sunflower seeds
20g (¾oz) chopped mixed candied peel
20g (¾oz) sultanas
25g (1oz) natural glacé cherries, roughly chopped
40g (1½oz) flaked almonds, lightly crushed
15g (½oz) plain flour

TO FINISH
125g (4oz) plain dark chocolate, in pieces

Enticing, chewy biscuits rich with dried fruit, nuts and sunflower seeds, and coated underneath with melted chocolate. For contrast, base-coat half the florentines in plain and half in white chocolate.

1 Preheat the oven to 180°C (160°C fan oven) mark 4. Melt the butter in a small heavy-based pan. Add the sugar and heat gently until dissolved, then bring to the boil. Take off the heat and stir in the cream, sunflower seeds, candied peel, sultanas, cherries, almonds and flour. Mix well until evenly combined.
2 Put heaped teaspoonfuls of the mixture on two lightly greased large baking sheets, spacing well apart to allow plenty of room for spreading.
3 Bake, one sheet at a time, for about 6–8 minutes until the biscuits have spread considerably and the edges are golden brown. Using a large plain metal biscuit cutter, push the edges into the centre to create neat rounds. Bake for a further 2 minutes or until deep golden. Leave on the baking sheet for 2 minutes, then transfer to a wire rack to cool completely.
4 Melt the chocolate in a heatproof bowl over a pan of simmering water; stir until smooth. Spread melted chocolate on the underside of each florentine and mark wavy lines with a fork. Put, chocolate-side up, on a sheet of non-stick baking parchment until set. Store in an airtight tin.

CHOCOLATE CHIP COOKIES

PREPARATION TIME: 15 minutes, plus cooling
COOKING TIME: 12–15 minutes
PER COOKIE: 200 cals; 10g fat; 26g carbohydrate

MAKES 18

125g (4oz) unsalted butter, softened

125g (4oz) golden caster sugar

1 egg

1 tsp vanilla extract

125g (4oz) porridge oats

150g (5oz) plain flour

½ tsp baking powder

200g (7oz) plain dark chocolate, cut into 1cm
    (½in) chunks

Crumbly and richly flavoured with chunks of chocolate, these large biscuits resemble American-style cookies. Don't be tempted to bake them until crisp or you will ruin their characteristic texture – the cookies will firm up as they cool.

1 Preheat the oven to 180°C (160°C fan oven) mark 4. Cream the butter and sugar together in a bowl until pale and creamy. Add the egg, vanilla extract and oats.

2 Sift the flour and baking powder together over the mixture and mix until evenly combined. Stir in the chocolate chunks.

3 Put dessertspoonfuls of the mixture on two lightly greased baking sheets, spacing them well apart to allow room for spreading. Flatten each one slightly with the back of a fork.

4 Bake for 12–15 minutes until risen and turning golden, but still quite soft. Leave on the baking sheet for 5 minutes, then transfer to a wire rack to cool. Store in an airtight tin for up to 1 week.

TO FREEZE: Bake the cookies and allow to cool. Once cold, pack and freeze in a freezerproof container. To use, thaw the cookies individually, as needed, at room temperature for an hour or two.

VARIATION: For dark chocolate cookies, replace 15g (½oz) of the flour with cocoa powder.

WHITE AND DARK CHOCOLATE COOKIES

PREPARATION TIME: 15 minutes, plus chilling
COOKING TIME: 10–12 minutes
PER COOKIE: 140 cals; 7g fat; 17g carbohydrate

MAKES 26

125g (4oz) unsalted butter, softened

125g (4oz) golden caster sugar

2 medium eggs, beaten

2 tsp vanilla extract

250g (9oz) self-raising flour, sifted

Finely grated zest of 1 orange

100g (3½oz) white chocolate, roughly chopped

100g (3½oz) dark chocolate, roughly chopped

Cookies are easy to make and everyone loves them – especially children. Make a batch and freeze any that are unlikely to be eaten within a couple of days. Simply remove a handful from the freezer as needed, to replenish the cookie tin. These cookies are particularly good with mugs of steaming hot chocolate.

1 Preheat the oven to 180°C (160°C fan oven) mark 4. Cream the butter and sugar together in a bowl until pale and creamy. Gradually beat in the eggs and vanilla extract.

2 Sift in the flour, add the orange zest, then sprinkle in the white and dark chocolate pieces. Mix the dough together with your hands.

3 Knead lightly, then wrap in clingfilm. Chill the cookie mixture for at least 30 minutes.

4 Divide the mixture into 26 pieces, roll each into a ball and flatten slightly to make a disc. Using a palette knife, transfer the discs to two or three large greased baking sheets, spacing them well apart. Bake for 10–12 minutes or until golden, but still fairly soft.

5 Leave on the baking sheets for 5 minutes, then transfer to a wire rack to cool completely.

TO FREEZE: Bake the cookies and allow to cool. Once cold, pack and freeze in a freezerproof container. To use, thaw the cookies individually, as needed, at room temperature for an hour or two.

CHERRY CHIP COOKIES

PREPARATION TIME: 20 minutes, plus cooling
COOKING TIME: 10–12 minutes
PER COOKIE: 210 cals; 9g fat; 31g carbohydrate

MAKES 12

75g (3oz) unsalted butter
25g (1oz) golden caster sugar
50g (2oz) light muscovado sugar
Few drops of vanilla extract
1 large egg, lightly beaten
175g (6oz) self-raising flour, sifted
Finely grated zest of 1 orange
125g (4oz) white chocolate, roughly chopped
125g (4oz) natural glacé cherries, roughly chopped
Icing sugar to dust

Scrumptious cookies – dotted with chunks of white chocolate and chopped glacé cherries – that will keep well in the biscuit tin for up to 3 days.

1 Preheat the oven to 180°C (160°C fan oven) mark 4. In a large bowl, beat together the butter, caster sugar, muscovado sugar and vanilla extract until well combined, using an electric whisk. Gradually beat in the egg until the mixture is light and fluffy.

2 With a metal spoon, lightly fold in the flour, orange zest, chopped chocolate and glacé cherries. Put tablespoonfuls of the mixture on to greased baking sheets and bake for 10–12 minutes. The cookies should be soft under a crisp crust.

3 Leave the cookies on the baking sheet for 1 minute, then transfer them to a wire rack. Dust with icing sugar just before serving.

COOK'S TIP: Glacé cherries that have been preserved naturally are dark red in colour and far superior to the familiar bright red version that contains artificial colouring and additives. Natural glacé cherries are available from selected supermarkets and delicatessens.

4

SPECIAL OCCASION CAKES

CHOCOLATE CHOUX BUNS

WHITE CHOCOLATE AND MACADAMIA NUT BROWNIES

PECAN FUDGE BROWNIES

SACHERTORTE

COSMIC CHOCOLATE CAKE

RICH CHOCOLATE MOUSSE CAKE

CHOCOLATE BRANDY TORTE

CHOCOLATE AND BANANA ROLL

CHOCOLATE ROULADE

TWO-TONE CHOCOLATE CAKE

CHOCOLATE AND GRAND MARNIER CAKE

CHOCOLATE CAKE WITH CHERRY TOPPING

CHOCOLATE RIBBON CAKE

ULTRA-DARK CHOCOLATE CAKE WITH RASPBERRIES

THE BEST CHOCOLATE CAKE IN THE WORLD

CHOCOLATE CHOUX BUNS

PREPARATION TIME: 25 minutes, plus cooling
COOKING TIME: 40–45 minutes
PER BUN: 470 cals; 39g fat; 26g carbohydrate

MAKES 8

65g (2½oz) plain flour
Pinch of salt
50g (2oz) butter, cut into cubes
150ml (¼ pint) sparkling spring water
1 level tbsp golden caster sugar
2 medium eggs, lightly beaten

FILLING
284ml carton double cream
1 tsp vanilla extract
1 level tsp golden caster sugar

TOPPING
200g (7oz) plain chocolate, in pieces
75g (3oz) butter, at room temperature

Light, moist choux buns filled with vanilla-flavoured cream and topped with melted chocolate...who could resist them?

1 Preheat the oven to 220°C (200°C fan oven) mark 7. Sift the flour with the salt on to a sheet of greaseproof paper. Put the butter, sparkling water and caster sugar in a medium heavy-based pan. Heat gently until the butter is melted and the sugar dissolved, then bring to a rapid boil.

2 Take off the heat and immediately tip in all the flour. Beat thoroughly with a wooden spoon until the mixture forms a smooth ball in the centre of the pan. Turn into a bowl and leave to cool for 15 minutes.

3 Add the eggs to the mixture, a little at a time, beating well after each addition. Make sure that the mixture is thick and shiny before adding any more egg – if it's added too quickly, the choux paste will become thin. Add just enough egg to give a smooth, dropping consistency (you may not need all of it).

4 Sprinkle a non-stick baking sheet with a little water. Using two dampened tablespoons, spoon the choux paste into 8 large mounds on the baking sheet, spacing them well apart to allow room for them to expand.

5 Bake for about 30 minutes until risen and golden brown. Take out the buns and turn off the oven. Make a small hole in the side of each bun, then put in the switched-off oven for 10–15 minutes to dry out. Transfer to a wire rack and set aside to cool.

6 To make the filling, whip the cream with the vanilla extract and sugar to soft peaks. Split the choux buns and fill them with the flavoured cream.

7 For the topping, melt the chocolate with the butter in a heatproof bowl over a pan of simmering water. Allow to cool until beginning to thicken. Top the choux buns with the warm melted chocolate to serve.

WHITE CHOCOLATE AND MACADAMIA NUT BROWNIES

PREPARATION TIME: 20 minutes, plus cooling
COOKING TIME: 30–35 minutes
PER BROWNIE: 490 cals; 20g fat; 29g carbohydrate

MAKES 12

75g (3oz) butter, plus extra to grease
500g (1lb 2oz) white chocolate, roughly chopped
3 large eggs
175g (6oz) golden caster sugar
175g (6oz) self-raising flour
Pinch of salt
175g (6oz) macadamia nuts, roughly chopped
1 tsp vanilla extract

If you like classic chocolate brownies, then you will adore this white chocolate version. Laden with chocolate and dotted with pieces of buttery macadamia nuts, they are absolutely divine. Macadamia nuts have a soft texture that works particularly well here, but you can, of course, use other nuts, such as pecans, hazelnuts or brazil nuts.

1 Preheat the oven to 190°C (170°C fan oven) mark 5. Grease and line a baking tin, measuring 19x27cm (7½x10½in) across the base (or use a tin with similar dimensions).

2 Put 100g (4oz) of the white chocolate in a heatproof bowl with the butter. Put over a pan of gently simmering water and leave until melted. Leave to cool slightly.

3 Whisk the eggs and sugar together in a large bowl until smooth, then gradually beat in the melted chocolate mixture; the consistency will become quite firm. Sift the flour and salt over the mixture, then fold in together with the nuts, chopped chocolate and vanilla extract.

4 Turn the mixture into the prepared tin and level the surface. Bake for 30–35 minutes until risen and golden, and the centre is just firm to the touch. Leave to cool in the tin. Turn out and cut into squares. Store in an airtight container for up to 1 week.

COOK'S TIP: When you remove the brownie from the oven, the mixture will still be soft under the crust; it firms up on cooling.

PECAN FUDGE BROWNIES

PREPARATION TIME: 30 minutes, plus cooling
COOKING TIME: 45–50 minutes
PER BROWNIE: 820 cals; 61g fat; 59g carbohydrate

MAKES 12

225g (8oz) unsalted butter, plus extra to grease
150g (5oz) plain, dark chocolate with 70% cocoa solids,
    in pieces
75g (3oz) plain chocolate (semi-sweet eg Bournville),
    in pieces
4 medium eggs
200g (7oz) golden caster sugar
175g (6oz) plain flour, sifted
2 tsp vanilla extract
175g (6oz) pecan nuts, roughly chopped

TOPPING
50g (2oz) unsalted butter, at room temperature
125g (4oz) light muscovado sugar
142ml carton single cream
1 tsp vanilla extract
175g (6oz) pecan nuts, medium chopped

WHITE CHOCOLATE SAUCE
200g (7oz) white chocolate
284ml carton single cream
3–4 tbsp white rum (optional)

TO FINISH
Cocoa powder to dust

Deliciously rich, nutty brownies, with a caramelised fudgey topping and a wicked white chocolate sauce. For a lighter alternative, serve with crème fraîche rather than the white chocolate sauce.

1 Preheat the oven to 180°C (160°C fan oven) mark 4. Grease and line the base of a 23cm (9in) square cake tin, 4cm (1½in) deep, with non-stick baking parchment.

2 Put the butter and both types of chocolate in a heatproof bowl over a pan of simmering water. Leave until the chocolate is melted, then remove from the heat and stir until smooth. Allow to cool.

3 Using an electric whisk, whisk the eggs and sugar together until thick and pale. Stir in the cooled chocolate mixture. Lightly fold in the flour, vanilla extract and chopped pecan nuts.

4 Pour the mixture into the prepared cake tin and bake for 45–50 minutes or until the brownie is almost cooked in the middle. Test by inserting a skewer in the centre – it should come out hot but with a little of the mixture still sticking to it. (The brownies continue to cook after they come out of the oven.) Leave to cool in the tin for 20–30 minutes.

5 For the topping, put the butter, muscovado sugar, single cream and vanilla extract in a saucepan. Heat slowly until the butter is melted and the sugar dissolved, then bring to the boil. Reduce the heat and simmer for 3–4 minutes. Add the chopped pecan nuts and pour the topping over the cooled brownie. Put under a hot grill for 1–2 minutes or until the topping starts to bubble and the nuts turn brown.

6 Meanwhile, make the sauce. Put the white chocolate and cream in a heatproof bowl over a saucepan of barely simmering water until the chocolate is melted. Remove from the heat, stir until smooth and allow to cool. Add the rum, if using.

7 To serve, cut the brownie into squares and dust with cocoa powder. Serve with the white chocolate sauce.

SACHERTORTE

PREPARATION TIME: 35 minutes, plus cooling
COOKING TIME: 45–55 minutes
PER SLICE (FOR 12): 540 cals; 37g fat;
43g carbohydrate
PER SLICE (FOR 16): 410 cals; 28g fat;
32g carbohydrate

MAKES 12–16 SLICES

175g (6oz) unsalted butter, at room temperature,
    plus extra to grease
225g (8oz) plain, dark chocolate
    with 70% cocoa solids, in pieces
175g (6oz) golden caster sugar
5 medium eggs, lightly beaten
3 level tbsp cocoa powder
125g (4oz) self-raising flour
4 tbsp brandy

GANACHE COATING
175g (6oz) plain chocolate, in pieces
75g (3oz) butter
4 tbsp double cream, warmed

TO DECORATE
12 lilac sugar-coated almonds, or 50g (2oz) milk
    chocolate, melted

A deliciously rich, moist cake, spiked with brandy and coated with chocolate ganache. Top with lilac sugared almonds, or a zig-zag drizzle of melted chocolate, for an elegant finish.

1 Preheat the oven to 190°C (170°C fan oven) mark 5. Grease and line a 20cm (8in) springform cake tin with non-stick baking parchment. Melt the chocolate in a heatproof bowl over a pan of simmering water. Take off the heat, stir until smooth and leave to cool for 5 minutes.

2 Cream together the butter and sugar, using a free-standing electric mixer (if you have one), until pale and fluffy. Gradually beat in two thirds of the beaten eggs – don't worry if the mixture curdles.

3 Sift in the cocoa powder together with 3 tbsp of the flour, then gradually beat in the remaining eggs. Fold in the rest of the flour. Pour in the melted chocolate and fold in, using a large metal spoon, until evenly incorporated. Add 2 tbsp of the brandy and stir to combine.

4 Put the mixture into the prepared cake tin, spread evenly and bake for 45 minutes, covering the tin loosely with foil if the cake appears to be browning too quickly. To test, insert a skewer into the centre of the cake; it should come out clean; if necessary, cook for an extra 5–10 minutes. Leave the cake to cool in the tin for 30 minutes.

5 Remove the cake from the tin and put on a wire rack. Leave until cold, then drizzle with the remaining brandy.

6 To make the chocolate ganache coating, melt the chocolate in a heatproof bowl over a pan of simmering water. Add the butter and the warm cream and stir everything together until smooth.

7 Position the wire rack over a tray and ladle the warm ganache coating over the top of the cake, letting it trickle down the sides. Use a palette knife to spread the ganache evenly over the cake.

8 Decorate with sugar-coated almonds, or a zig-zag drizzle of melted chocolate (see page 12). Allow to set, then store in an airtight container. Eat within 1 week.

TO FREEZE: Either freeze the unfinished cake at step 5 in the usual way, or open-freeze the ganache-coated cake at the end of step 7 (without wrapping). Once frozen, double wrap the cake with freezer film and freeze for up to 1 month. To use, allow the cake to thaw at cool room temperature for 5 hours.

COSMIC CHOCOLATE CAKE

PREPARATION TIME: 30 minutes,
plus overnight chilling
COOKING TIME: 45–55 minutes
PER SLICE: 450 cals; 32g fat; 35g carbohydrate

MAKES 20 SLICES

450g (1lb) golden granulated sugar
450g (1lb) plain, dark chocolate
    with 60–70% cocoa solids, roughly chopped
450g (1lb) butter, roughly chopped
6 large eggs
150g (5oz) plain flour

TO ASSEMBLE

142ml carton whipping cream
Cocoa powder, sifted, to dust
Piped chocolate stars (see page 12), plus a little melted
    chocolate (optional)

This delectable cake has the texture of a chocolate mousse. A slice is worth every calorie!

1 Preheat the oven to 180°C (160°C fan oven) mark 4. Base-line two 23cm (9in) spring-release cake tins with greaseproof paper.

2 Dissolve the sugar in 150ml (5fl oz) water in a large saucepan over a low heat, then bring to the boil and bubble for 1 minute. Add the chocolate and butter, stirring until melted. Remove from the heat.

3 Lightly whisk the eggs in a bowl. Add the flour and whisk until smooth. Add to the chocolate mixture and stir until well combined.

4 Pour the mixture into the prepared tins and put each one in a roasting tray containing enough warm water to come halfway up the sides of the tins. Bake for 45–55 minutes or until firm, transposing the roasting tins halfway through to ensure even cooking, and topping up the water if necessary. The cakes should be firm to the touch in the centre.

5 Leave in the tins to cool for about 1 hour, then turn out on to wire racks lined with greaseproof paper. Peel off the lining paper. When the cakes are cold, cover with clingfilm and refrigerate overnight.

6 Whip the cream until thick and use to sandwich the two cakes together. Dust the top with cocoa. If using the chocolate stars, dip a point of each one into melted chocolate and arrange at an angle on top of the cake.

RICH CHOCOLATE MOUSSE CAKE

PREPARATION TIME: 20 minutes
COOKING TIME: 45 minutes–1 hour
PER SLICE (FOR 6): 550 cals; 45g fat;
25g carbohydrate
PER SLICE (FOR 12): 280 cals; 22g fat;
12g carbohydrate

MAKES 6 OR 12 SLICES

200g (7oz) plain, dark chocolate
　　with 60–70% cocoa solids, in pieces
1 level tsp instant coffee granules
100ml (4fl oz) double cream
1 tbsp brandy
3 large eggs
50g (2oz) golden caster sugar

TOPPING

175g (6oz) plain, dark chocolate
　　with 60–70% cocoa solids, in pieces
75ml (3fl oz) double cream
25g (1oz) butter

This adaptable, melt-in-the-mouth, rich chocolate cake is easy to make and freezes to perfection. Cut it into slim rectangles and serve with coffee, or with pouring cream or a thin fresh vanilla custard, as a dessert. Alternatively, cut into small squares, slip it into petits fours cases and serve as a finale to a special meal.

1　Preheat the oven to 180°C (160°C fan oven) mark 4. Grease and base-line a 16cm (6½in) square cake tin, 4cm (1½in) deep, with non-stick baking parchment.

2　Put the chocolate and instant coffee in a small heatproof bowl over a pan of simmering water and leave until melted. Take off the heat, stir until smooth and allow to cool.

3　Whip the double cream until it just holds its shape, then whisk in the brandy.

4　Whisk the eggs and sugar together in another bowl until pale in colour and thick. Fold in the melted chocolate, followed by the cream, making sure the ingredients are thoroughly combined. Pour the mixture into the prepared tin.

5　Stand the cake tin in a roasting tray and pour in enough hot water to come at least halfway up the sides of the tin. Bake for 45 minutes–1 hour or until just firm to the centre; a crust will form on the top, so you will need to press this gently to feel how firm the cake is underneath. Leave to cool in the tin.

6　To make the topping, put the chocolate and cream in a small heavy-based pan over a low heat and stir until melted. Add the butter, again stirring until melted. Allow to cool, stirring occasionally, until thickened to a spreadable consistency.

7　Turn the cake out on to a board and spread the topping evenly over the top. Chill until just firm, then remove from the fridge. Serve the cake at room temperature, otherwise the topping may be too solid. Using a sharp knife, cut into 6 slices, or 12 small squares to serve.

TO FREEZE: Wrap and freeze the finished cake. To use, thaw at cool room temperature for 1–2 hours, then slice.

CHOCOLATE BRANDY TORTE

PREPARATION TIME: 10 minutes, plus cooling
COOKING TIME: 45 minutes
PER SLICE (FOR 6): 580 cals; 40g fat;
43g carbohydrate
PER SLICE (FOR 8): 440 cals; 30g fat;
32g carbohydrate

MAKES 6–8 SLICES

125g (4oz) butter, diced, plus extra to grease
225g (8oz) plain, dark chocolate
    with 60–70% cocoa solids, in pieces
3 large eggs, separated
125g (4oz) light muscovado sugar
50ml (2fl oz) brandy
75g (3oz) self-raising flour, sifted
50g (2oz) ground almonds

TO FINISH

Icing sugar to dust

The appealing cracked, crusted surface to this wonderful torte conceals a soft, moist-textured cake beneath. The torte can be prepared and cooked within the hour – a dusting of icing sugar is all that is required to finish.

1 Preheat the oven to 180°C (160°C fan oven) mark 4. Grease and base-line a 20cm (8in) springform cake tin.
2 Put the diced butter and chocolate pieces in a bowl and set over a pan of simmering water to melt. Stir until smooth. Remove from the heat and set aside to cool slightly.
3 Whisk the egg yolks and muscovado sugar together until pale and creamy, then whisk in the brandy and melted chocolate on a low speed. Fold in the flour and ground almonds, with a large metal spoon. Put the mixture to one side.
4 Whisk the egg whites in a clean bowl to the soft peak stage. Beat a large spoonful of the egg white into the chocolate mixture to lighten it, then carefully fold in the remainder with a large metal spoon.
5 Pour the mixture into the prepared tin and bake for 45 minutes, or until a skewer inserted into the centre comes out clean. Leave the cake to cool in the tin for 10 minutes, then turn it out on to a wire rack. Remove the lining paper from the base of the cake when it's completely cold.
6 To serve, simply dust the top of the cake with sifted icing sugar.

TO FREEZE: Complete the recipe (to the end of step 5). Wrap in a freezer bag and freeze for up to 1 month. To use, thaw the torte at cool room temperature for 2 hours. Dust with sifted icing sugar to serve.

CHOCOLATE AND BANANA ROLL

PREPARATION TIME: 40 minutes, plus cooling
COOKING TIME: 25 minutes
PER SLICE: 450 cals; 31g fat; 33g carbohydrate

MAKES 6 SLICES

4 level tbsp cocoa powder

150ml (¼ pint) semi-skimmed milk

5 medium eggs, separated

125g (4oz) golden caster sugar, plus 2 level tbsp to dust

FILLING

250g tub mascarpone

1 tbsp maple syrup

3 tbsp double cream

1 banana, peeled and sliced

1 tsp vanilla extract

TO FINISH

Golden caster sugar to dust

This fabulously squidgy chocolate roll with its creamy banana filling can be assembled up to 3 hours before serving. It's excellent as a pudding, or you can serve it as a teatime treat if you prefer.

1 Preheat the oven to 180°C (160°C fan oven) mark 4. Line a 30x20cm (12x8in) Swiss roll tin with non-stick baking parchment.
2 Mix the cocoa powder with 3 tbsp milk to a paste in a medium bowl. Heat the remaining milk in a small pan until almost boiling, then slowly pour on to the cocoa paste, stirring well. Leave to cool for 10 minutes.
3 Put the egg yolks and caster sugar into a large bowl or mixer and whisk until pale, thick and mousse-like. Gradually whisk in the cooled chocolate milk.
4 Put the egg whites into a dry, clean grease-free bowl and whisk until stiff peaks form. Gently fold one third into the chocolate mixture to loosen it slightly, then carefully fold in the rest.
5 Spoon the mixture into the prepared tin and smooth the surface, using a palette knife. Bake for 25 minutes until risen and just firm to the touch.
6 Turn the cake out on to a sheet of baking parchment dusted with caster sugar, then peel off the lining parchment. Cover with a clean, warm, damp tea-towel to prevent the sponge from drying out as it cools.
7 To make the filling, put the mascarpone in a bowl, add the maple syrup and cream, and stir well. Put the sliced banana in a separate bowl and sprinkle with the vanilla extract; toss to mix.
8 To assemble, uncover the sponge and, using a palette knife, spread half of the mascarpone mixture evenly over the surface. Scatter the banana slices on top. Starting at a short edge and using the parchment to help you, gently roll up the cake. Slide it on to a large plate and dust with caster sugar. Serve accompanied by the remaining flavoured mascarpone.

TO PREPARE AHEAD: Make the cake to the end of step 6 and cover the damp cloth with clingfilm. Set aside in a cool place for up to 24 hours. Continue as above.

CHOCOLATE ROULADE

PREPARATION TIME: 30 minutes,
plus cooling and chilling
COOKING TIME: 25 minutes
PER SERVING: 330 cals; 23g fat; 35g carbohydrate

MAKES 10 SLICES

175g (6oz) plain, dark chocolate
    with 60–70% cocoa solids, in pieces
6 large eggs, separated
175g (6oz) golden caster sugar

FILLING
284ml carton whipping cream
1 level tsp golden caster sugar, plus extra to dust
½ tsp vanilla extract

TO FINISH
Cocoa powder to sprinkle
Chocolate curls (page 10) to decorate

Few chocolate concoctions taste as good as a perfectly cooked, classic chocolate roulade. With the texture of a baked chocolate mousse, it should literally melt in the mouth. Serve as a dessert, or with coffee.

1 Preheat the oven to 180°C (160°C fan oven) mark 4. Line a 38x28cm (15x11in) non-stick Swiss roll tin with non-stick baking parchment.

2 Put the chocolate in a small heatproof bowl with 150ml (¼ pint) water. Melt slowly over a pan of gently simmering water. Take off the heat, stir until smooth and set aside to cool slightly.

3 Put the egg yolks and caster sugar in a bowl and beat with an electric whisk until light in colour and thick. Beat in the warm, liquid chocolate until thoroughly blended.

4 In a clean bowl, whisk the egg whites until they just hold soft peaks. Beat a quarter of the egg white into the chocolate mixture to loosen it, then carefully fold in the remainder using a large metal spoon, until evenly combined; do not over-fold. Pour immediately into the prepared tin.

5 Bake for about 25 minutes (see cook's tip). Allow the roulade to cool a little in the tin, then cover with a clean, warm damp tea-towel. Once cold, cover the cloth with clingfilm; refrigerate for at least 6 hours or overnight.

6 Whip the cream in a bowl until it is just beginning to thicken. Add 1 level tsp caster sugar and the vanilla extract. Continue to whip until it just holds its shape.

7 Lightly dust a large sheet of greaseproof paper with caster sugar. Remove the clingfilm and cloth from the roulade and carefully turn out on to the greaseproof paper. Cut 5mm (¼in) off two short sides of the roulade to neaten. Spread the cream over the roulade and roll up tightly from the long side, using greaseproof paper to help – don't worry if the sponge cracks.

8 Transfer to a serving dish, sprinkle with cocoa and decorate with chocolate curls to serve.

COOK'S TIP: A crust develops on the surface during baking, so it's difficult to see if the roulade is cooked. Press the centre lightly with your fingertips – the sponge should spring back.

TO PREPARE AHEAD: Make the roulade (to the end of step 7) up to 6 hours ahead or overnight, then cover and refrigerate. Finish as above.
TO FREEZE: Make the roulade (to the end of step 7), wrap and freeze. To use, thaw at cool room temperature overnight. Finish as above.

TWO-TONE CHOCOLATE CAKE

PREPARATION TIME: 50 minutes,
plus cooling and chilling
COOKING TIME: 40–45 minutes
PER SLICE (FOR 14): 470 cals; 35g fat;
34g carbohydrate
PER SLICE (FOR 16): 420 cals; 31g fat;
30g carbohydrate

MAKES 14–16 SLICES

125g (4oz) butter, plus extra to grease
125g (4oz) plain, dark chocolate with 70% cocoa solids,
    in pieces
150g (5oz) golden caster sugar
3 large eggs, separated
100g (3½oz) ground almonds
100g (3½oz) day-old breadcrumbs

WHITE GANACHE FILLING
225g (8oz) good quality white chocolate, in pieces
200ml (7fl oz) double cream

DARK GANACHE TOPPING
75g (3oz) plain, dark chocolate with 70% cocoa solids,
    in pieces
15g (½oz) butter
100ml (4fl oz) double cream

TO FINISH
White chocolate curls to decorate (see page 10)
Icing sugar to dust

This luscious, rich, moist cake owes its light texture to fresh breadcrumbs, which take the place of flour. A white chocolate ganache filling and dark ganache topping make it sensational.

1 Preheat the oven to 180°C (160°C fan oven) mark 4. Grease and base-line a 25x15cm (10x6in) shallow rectangular cake tin with non-stick baking parchment.

2 To make the cake, put the chocolate in a small, heavy-based saucepan with 6 tbsp water. Melt over a low heat, stirring, until smooth. Allow to cool.

3 Put the butter in a large bowl and beat until soft and creamy. Gradually beat in the caster sugar until pale and fluffy. Beat in the egg yolks, one at a time, then add the cooled chocolate mixture, ground almonds and breadcrumbs and fold in gently until evenly combined.

4 Whisk the egg whites in a clean bowl until they form soft peaks, then stir one quarter into the chocolate mixture to loosen it. Carefully fold in the remainder.

5 Pour the mixture into the prepared tin and smooth the surface. Bake for 40–45 minutes or until just firm in the centre. Allow to cool in the tin for 15 minutes, then carefully turn out on to a wire rack to cool completely.

6 To make the white chocolate ganache, put the chocolate in a heatproof bowl with the cream. Set over a saucepan of barely simmering water until the chocolate has melted. Stir until smooth, allow to cool, then chill for about 30 minutes to firm up slightly. Finally, whisk until thick and pale in colour; it should be the consistency of whipped double cream.

7 Put the cooled cake on a board and, using a sharp bread knife, carefully split it in two horizontally. Carefully lift off the top layer. Spoon the white chocolate mixture on to the bottom layer, smooth it over with a palette knife and position the other cake layer on top, pressing down lightly.

8 To prepare the dark chocolate ganache, put the chocolate, butter and cream in a small pan and stir over a gentle heat until melted and smooth. While it's still warm, pour the ganache on top of the cake and smooth with a palette knife. Chill for 30 minutes or until the topping is just set.

9 Decorate with white chocolate curls and dust with icing sugar. Cut into squares or rectangles to serve.

TO FREEZE: Prepare to the end of step 8; wrap and freeze. Thaw at cool room temperature overnight, then apply the decoration.

CHOCOLATE AND GRAND MARNIER CAKE

PREPARATION TIME: 50 minutes,
plus cooling and chilling
COOKING TIME: 50 minutes
PER SLICE (FOR 8): 800 cals; 56g fat;
60g carbohydrate
PER SLICE (FOR 10): 640 cals; 45g fat;
48g carbohydrate

MAKES 8–10 SLICES

125g (4oz) unsalted butter, softened, plus extra to grease
225g (8oz) plain, dark chocolate
    with 60–70% cocoa solids, in pieces
5 large eggs, separated
150g (5oz) golden caster sugar
4 tbsp Grand Marnier, or other orange liqueur

MOUSSE
142ml carton double cream
225g (8oz) plain chocolate (semi-sweet eg Bournville)
4 large eggs, separated

TO FINISH
Cocoa powder to dust
175g (6oz) good quality white chocolate, in pieces

This stunning mousse cake with its white chocolate filigree collar is easier to make than it looks, though the collar can be omitted.

1 Preheat the oven to 180°C (160°C fan oven) mark 4. Grease a 20cm (8in) spring-release cake tin and line with non-stick baking parchment. Put the plain chocolate in a heatproof bowl over a pan of simmering water and leave until melted; stir until smooth. Take off the heat.

2 Whisk the egg yolks and sugar together in a heatproof bowl over a pan of hot water for about 3 minutes until the mixture is thick and creamy. Continue whisking, adding the softened butter a little at a time, then lower the whisk setting to slow and whisk in the melted dark chocolate.

3 Whisk the egg whites in a clean bowl to soft peaks, then carefully fold into the mixture, using a large metal spoon. Pour into the prepared tin and bake for 50 minutes or until risen and the top is beginning to crack. Leave to cool in the tin for 1 hour; the cake will sink a little.

4 Remove the cake from the tin and slice horizontally into two layers. Put the top layer, cut-side up, back in the tin and drizzle with half the liqueur. Drizzle the remaining liqueur over the bottom layer; set aside.

5 To make the mousse, lightly whip the cream and set aside. Melt the chocolate (as in step 1), allow to cool a little, then beat in the egg yolks. Fold in the whipped cream. Whisk the egg whites in a clean bowl to soft peaks, then fold into the chocolate mixture. Spoon over the cake layer in the tin, spreading it to the edges. Chill for 3 hours or overnight.

6 Position the other cake layer, cut-side down, on top of the mousse. Carefully remove the cake from the tin and smooth the edges with a round-bladed knife. Dust the top with cocoa and put on a serving plate.

7 To make the collar, measure the height of the cake and cut a strip of non-stick baking parchment that will fit comfortably around it – about 66cm (26in) long and 6.5cm (2¾in) high. Cut a second strip to fit around the cake but 5cm (2in) higher than the cake. Melt 50g (2oz) white chocolate and spread over the narrower strip of baking parchment to cover it.

8 Leave to firm up a little; the chocolate should be shiny and pliable, but not liquid. Carefully wrap, chocolate-side inwards, around the cake.

9 Refrigerate the cake for about 20 minutes until the chocolate collar is set, then carefully peel away the parchment. Spread the remaining chocolate over two thirds of the width of the second parchment strip and, drizzling the chocolate from a spoon, make a zigzag pattern over the top one third. Repeat the process (in step 8) to apply this collar to the cake. Refrigerate until firm, or up to 24 hours. To serve, carefully peel away the parchment.

TO FREEZE: Prepare to the end of step 6, then wrap and freeze (without the collar). To use, thaw overnight in the fridge, then complete the recipe.

CHOCOLATE CAKE WITH CHERRY TOPPING

PREPARATION TIME: 1 hour,
plus marinating and chilling
COOKING TIME: 30–35 minutes
PER SLICE (FOR 10): 650 cals; 52g fat;
34g carbohydrate
PER SLICE (FOR 12): 540 cals; 43g fat;
29g carbohydrate

MAKES 10–12 SLICES

350g (12oz) pitted fresh cherries, or 400g pitted cherries
    from a jar or can, drained
3 tbsp dark rum
125g (4oz) butter, softened, plus extra to grease
50g (2oz) blanched almonds
50g (2oz) plain flour
125g (4oz) plain, dark chocolate with 70% cocoa solids,
    in pieces
3 large eggs, separated
125g (4oz) golden caster sugar

GANACHE TOPPING

225g (8oz) plain, dark chocolate with 70% cocoa solids,
    chopped
450ml (¾ pint) double cream

TO DECORATE

Chocolate curls (see page 10)
Cocoa powder to dust

Rum-soaked cherries and rich, moist chocolate cake are a magical combination. If fresh cherries aren't available, full-flavoured bottled or canned morello cherries are an excellent alternative.

1 Put the cherries in a bowl and sprinkle with 2 tbsp rum. Cover and leave to marinate for 6 hours or overnight.

2 Preheat the oven to 180°C (160°C fan oven) mark 4. Grease and base-line a deep 23cm (9in) cake tin. Put the almonds on a baking sheet and toast under a preheated grill until golden brown. Cool, then put in a food processor with the flour and whiz until finely ground.

3 Melt the chocolate with 3 tbsp water in a bowl over a pan of simmering water. Remove from the heat and let cool slightly. Add the remaining rum and the egg yolks and beat until smooth.

4 Put the butter and sugar in a bowl and beat until light and fluffy. Stir in the chocolate mixture, then gently fold in the flour and almond mixture. Whisk the egg whites in a clean bowl to soft peaks, then fold into the chocolate mixture.

5 Pour the mixture into the prepared tin and bake for 30–35 minutes or until a skewer inserted into the centre comes out clean. Leave to cool in the tin for 10 minutes, then turn out on to a wire rack to cool completely.

6 For the ganache topping, put the chocolate in a heatproof bowl. Bring the cream to the boil in a small pan, then pour on to the chocolate and allow to stand for 5 minutes until the chocolate is melted. Stir until smooth and set aside to cool. Using an electric whisk, beat the ganache until paler in colour and thick.

7 Clean the cake tin and return the cake to the tin. Scatter the cherries, together with any juice, over the cake. Spoon the chocolate ganache on top, smooth the surface, then cover and refrigerate for at least 2 hours.

8 Decorate with chocolate curls and dust with cocoa. Serve cut into thin slices, with pouring cream and extra cherries, if wished.

TO PREPARE AHEAD: Make the cake and assemble to the end of step 7; store in an airtight container in the fridge for up to 3 days. To use, take it out of the fridge 30–45 minutes before serving to allow the chocolate topping to soften slightly. Finish as above.
TO FREEZE: Make the cake (to the end of step 7), pack and freeze. To use, defrost overnight at cool room temperature. Finish as above.

CHOCOLATE RIBBON CAKE

PREPARATION TIME: 30 minutes,
plus cooling and chilling
COOKING TIME: 50 minutes
PER SLICE: 760 cals; 60g fat; 44g carbohydrate

MAKES 10 SLICES

BISCUIT BASE

40g (1½oz) butter

2 level tsp cocoa powder

125g (4oz) shortbread biscuits

75g (3oz) milk chocolate hazelnuts (see cook's tip)

FILLING

125g (4oz) plain, dark chocolate with 70% cocoa solids,
   in pieces

125g (4oz) good quality white chocolate, in pieces

400g (14oz) full-fat cream cheese

125g (4oz) golden caster sugar

3 large eggs, beaten

142ml carton double cream

CUSTARD

142ml carton double cream

300ml (½ pint) semi-skimmed milk

1 vanilla pod, split

3 large egg yolks

50g (2oz) golden caster sugar

TO FINISH

Chocolate ribbons made with 125g (4oz) plain,
   dark chocolate with 70% cocoa solids
   (see page 11), optional

Cocoa powder to dust

Fresh orange segments to serve (optional)

Luxurious and rich, this cake is easy to cook and tastes fabulous. Chocolate ribbons add a stylish finish, though you could omit them and simply dust the top of the cake with cocoa if you prefer.

1 Base-line a 23cm (9in) spring-release cake tin (by wrapping foil over the base, then clipping it into position).

2 For the biscuit base, melt the butter in a small pan, add the cocoa and cook for 30 seconds. Put the biscuits in a food processor with the chocolate-coated hazelnuts and pulse until finely chopped. Stir in the butter mix, then spoon into the prepared tin, pressing down with the back of a spoon to make an even layer. Chill for 30 minutes. Preheat the oven to 180°C (160°C fan oven) mark 4.

3 For the filling, melt both types of chocolate separately in heatproof bowls over pans of gently simmering water; stir until smooth and let cool. Beat together the cream cheese and caster sugar in a large bowl until smooth. Gradually beat in the eggs, then the cream. Divide the mixture between two bowls. Stir the melted plain chocolate into one portion; stir the white chocolate into the other mixture.

4 Spoon the plain chocolate mixture on to the chilled biscuit base, then smooth with a palette knife. Cover with the white chocolate mixture and smooth again. Bake for 50 minutes or until the cake is golden, just set round the outside and starting to shrink away from the side of the tin. Switch off the oven and leave the cake to cool inside. Chill the cake in its tin for at least 2–3 hours.

5 To make the custard, put the cream and milk in a pan with the vanilla pod and bring to the boil. Beat together the egg yolks and sugar, then pour on the hot milk, stirring well. Return to the clean pan and cook over a very low heat, stirring continuously, until the custard thickens slightly; don't let the mixture boil, or it will curdle. Strain into a chilled bowl, cool and chill.

6 Unmould the chilled cake on to a serving plate. Arrange the chocolate ribbons if using on top, then dust with cocoa. Cut the cake into slices and serve with the vanilla custard, and fresh orange segments if you like.

COOK'S TIP: Buy chocolate-coated nuts, or break up a bar of chocolate with hazelnuts.

TO PREPARE AHEAD: Up to 2 days in advance, complete the recipe to the end of step 5, and make the ribbons (if using). Cover and chill the cake, custard and ribbons separately. To use, complete the recipe.

TO FREEZE: Cool, wrap and freeze the cake at the end of step 4. To use, thaw the cake overnight in the fridge, then complete the recipe.

ULTRA-DARK CHOCOLATE CAKE WITH RASPBERRIES

PREPARATION TIME: 15 minutes,
plus cooling and standing
COOKING TIME: 1 hour
PER SLICE: 370 cals; 24g fat; 34g carbohydrate

MAKES 16 SLICES

200g (7oz) butter, preferably unsalted, plus extra to
   grease
5 level tbsp plain white flour
1 level tsp baking powder
275g (10oz) plain, dark chocolate with 70% cocoa solids,
   in pieces
5 large eggs
225g (8oz) golden caster sugar

CHOCOLATE SAUCE
125g (4oz) golden syrup
175g (6oz) plain, dark chocolate with 70% cocoa solids,
   in pieces

TO FINISH
125–175g (4–6oz) raspberries
Chocolate-coated coffee beans
Chocolate curls (see page 10)

With its berries, cream and chocolate sauce, this cake is rich
enough to serve as a pudding. For a light-textured cake, it's best
to use a food mixer. You can serve the cake 2 or 3 hours after
baking, rather than leaving it to stand for 12 hours, but the
texture will be much more crumbly.

1 Preheat the oven to 170°C (150°C fan oven) mark 3. Base-line a 25cm
(10in) spring-release cake tin with non-stick baking parchment, then
lightly grease the sides. Sift together the flour and baking powder. Put the
chocolate and butter in a heatproof bowl and melt over a pan of gently
simmering water. Take off the heat, stir until smooth and allow to cool.

2 Put the eggs and sugar in a food mixer or large bowl and whisk until
very thick and mousse-like. Carefully fold in the cooled chocolate mix,
followed by the flour. Pour immediately into the prepared tin and bake
for 1 hour until a crust has formed on the surface. Test by inserting a thin
skewer into the centre; it should come out clean.

3 Leave the cake to cool in the tin for 5 minutes, then cover with a damp
cloth and leave to cool completely. Dampen the cloth again; put it on the
cake and cover with clingfilm. Leave to stand for up to 12 hours before
turning out.

4 To make the chocolate sauce, put the golden syrup in a pan with 200ml
(7fl oz) water. Add the chocolate and set over a gentle heat until the
chocolate is melted, then bring to the boil and simmer for 5 minutes.
Take off the heat and allow to cool (or you can use it warm if preferred).

5 Arrange the raspberries and coffee beans on top of the cake, then drizzle
with the sauce. Decorate with chocolate curls and cut into slices to serve.

TO PREPARE AHEAD: Up to 12 hours in advance, make the cake (to the
end of step 3). Make the chocolate sauce up to 3 days ahead. Cover and
chill the cake and sauce separately. To use, complete the recipe.
TO FREEZE: Complete the cake to the end of step 3; wrap and freeze.
Make the sauce and freeze in a suitable container. Thaw both cake and
sauce at cool room temperature for 4 hours. Complete the recipe.

THE BEST CHOCOLATE CAKE IN THE WORLD

PREPARATION TIME: 20 minutes
COOKING TIME: 1¼ hours
PER SLICE: 310 cals; 20g fat; 29g carbohydrate

MAKES 16 SLICES

125g (4oz) butter, cubed, plus extra to grease
200g (7oz) plain chocolate (semi-sweet eg Bournville),
    in pieces
8 medium eggs, separated
200g (7oz) golden caster sugar

CHOCOLATE GANACHE

100g (3½oz) plain chocolate (semi-sweet eg Bournville),
    in pieces
75ml (3fl oz) double cream
25g (1oz) butter

TO DECORATE

Simple chocolate curls made with 100g (3½oz) plain
    chocolate (see page 10)

This decadent, mouth-watering cake is perfect for a special occasion. There's no flour in the recipe, so the cake is more like a light, fudgey mousse covered with a rich ganache…heaven.

1 Preheat the oven to 180°C (160°C fan oven) mark 4. Grease and line a 23cm (9in) springform cake tin.

2 Melt the chocolate and butter in a heatproof bowl set over a pan of simmering water. Remove from the heat and allow to cool for a few minutes.

3 Put the egg yolks and sugar in a food mixer or large bowl and whisk until pale, thick and mousse-like, then whisk in the chocolate mixture.

4 Whisk the egg whites in a clean, grease-free bowl until soft peaks form. Add a third to the chocolate mixture and fold in, using a large metal spoon. Add the remaining whisked egg whites and fold in carefully.

5 Immediately pour the mixture into the prepared tin and bake for 1¼ hours. Turn off the oven. Cover the cake with a damp tea-towel and leave to cool in the oven; it will sink in the centre as it cools.

6 To make the ganache, put the chocolate, cream and butter in a bowl and melt in the microwave, allowing 1–2 minutes on High in a 900W model; mix well. (Alternatively melt the chocolate with the butter and cream in a heatproof bowl over a pan of simmering water.)

7 Take the cake out of the tin and peel off the lining paper. Put on a serving plate then ladle the ganache over the cake, so it covers the top and drizzles down the sides. Leave until just set. Using a palette knife, scatter the chocolate curls on top of the cake to serve.

VARIATION: For a simple finish, omit the chocolate curls and dust the top of the cake liberally with 2 tbsp each of cocoa powder and icing sugar.

5

SWEET TREATS

BRANDY TRUFFLES

GRAND MARNIER TRUFFLES

CHOCOLATE DIPPED FRUIT AND NUTS

CHOCOLATE NUT SLICE

CHOCOLATE FUDGE

CHOCOLATE EASTER EGG

SOLID CHOCOLATE EGGS

RICH CHOCOLATE SAUCE

CHOCOLATE FUDGE SAUCE

CHOCOLATE CRÈME ANGLAISE

CHOCOLATE GANACHE

CHOCOLATE FUDGE FROSTING

CHOCOLATE BUTTERCREAM

CHOCOLATE GLACÉ ICING

BRANDY TRUFFLES

PREPARATION TIME: 35 minutes,
plus overnight chilling
PER TRUFFLE: 90 cals; 8g fat; 3g carbohydrate

MAKES ABOUT 20–25

142ml carton thick double cream
½ vanilla pod
200g (7oz) plain, dark chocolate
   with 60–70% cocoa solids, in pieces
25g (1oz) unsalted butter, in pieces
2 tbsp brandy

TO FINISH
25g (1oz) cocoa powder to dust

Velvety smooth truffles, with a wonderful fudgey texture – pack into boxes for the ideal foody gift. Refrigerate for up to 5 days, but remove the truffles from the fridge an hour before serving to enjoy them at their best.

1 Pour the cream into a heavy-based pan. Split the vanilla pod and scrape the vanilla seeds into the pan; add the pod, too. Slowly bring to the boil, take off the heat and set aside to infuse for 20 minutes.
2 Melt the chocolate in a heatproof bowl over a pan of gently simmering water. Remove from the heat and beat in the butter.
3 Remove the vanilla pod from the cream and discard. Stir the infused cream into the chocolate mixture, with the brandy. Pour into a shallow tin, cover and chill overnight until firm.
4 Dust your hands with cocoa powder and shape the truffle mixture into balls. Roll in cocoa to coat and put on a baking sheet lined with non-stick baking parchment. Chill overnight, or until required.

GRAND MARNIER TRUFFLES

PREPARATION TIME: 40 minutes, plus chilling
PER TRUFFLE: 120 cals; 9g fat; 5g carbohydrate

MAKES ABOUT 20

175g (6oz) plain, dark chocolate
   with 70% cocoa solids, in pieces
100ml (4fl oz) double cream
Finely grated zest of ½ orange
4 tbsp Grand Marnier or other orange liqueur

TO FINISH
175g (6oz) plain chocolate
   with 50–60% cocoa solids, in pieces, to dip

Sensational, creamy truffles spiked with orange liqueur and a hint of orange zest. Vary the flavourings to taste. For mocha truffles, use Kahlua or Tia Maria and 1 tsp finely ground espresso coffee in place of the orange flavourings. If preferred, you can simply roll the truffles in cocoa powder, rather than dip them in chocolate.

1 Put the chocolate in a heatproof bowl. Pour the cream into a small pan and bring to the boil, then pour on to the chocolate and stir gently in one direction, until melted and smooth. Add the orange zest and liqueur and stir until well mixed. Allow to cool, then chill for about 15 minutes.
2 Beat the mixture for about 5 minutes until it has a fudge-like consistency. Using two teaspoons, shape the truffle mixture into small balls and put on a baking sheet lined with non-stick baking parchment. Or pipe small balls, using a piping bag fitted with a 1cm (½in) nozzle. Chill in the freezer for 1 hour.
3 Melt the chocolate for dipping in a heatproof bowl over a pan of simmering water; stir until smooth and leave to cool until thickened to a coating consistency. To coat each truffle, spear with a fork and dip into the melted chocolate, turning to coat evenly. Put the dipped truffles on a lined baking sheet and chill until set. Serve straight from the fridge.

CHOCOLATE DIPPED FRUIT AND NUTS

PREPARATION TIME: 20 minutes, plus setting
PER SERVING: 170 cals; 11g fat; 15g carbohydrate

SERVES 8

225g (8oz) strawberries
125g (4oz) physalis fruit
125g (4oz) kumquats
125g (4oz) red cherries
125g (4oz) grapes
50g (2oz) skinned Brazil nuts
150g (5oz) plain chocolate
    with 50–60% cocoa solids, in pieces, to dip

Elegant chocolate-dipped fruits and nuts add a decorative finish to cold desserts and smart cakes, or you can serve a selection in a glass serving bowl to round off a special meal.

1 Wash the fruit if necessary and pat dry thoroughly on kitchen paper, but don't remove the stems from the cherries or strawberries. Peel back the papery petals from the physalis fruit. Set aside with the nuts.
2 Put the chocolate for dipping in a heatproof bowl over a pan of simmering water to melt. Stir until smooth and leave to cool until thickened to a coating consistency.
3 Partially dip the fruits and nuts in the chocolate to half-coat, allowing the excess chocolate to drip back into the bowl. Put on a tray lined with non-stick baking parchment. Leave in a cool place or refrigerate until set.

VARIATION: Use good quality white or milk chocolate for dipping.

CHOCOLATE NUT SLICE

PREPARATION TIME: 20 minutes, plus chilling
PER SLICE: 70 cals; 5g fat; 3g carbohydrate

MAKES 30 SLICES

100g (3½oz) plain, dark chocolate
    with 70% cocoa solids, in pieces
40g (1½oz) unsalted butter
40g (1½oz) blanched almonds, finely chopped and
    toasted
15g (½oz) preserved stem ginger in syrup, drained and
    finely diced
25g (1oz) raisins, preferably lexia
2 tbsp brandy

TO FINISH

75g (3oz) white chocolate, in pieces
75g (3oz) flaked almonds, lightly crushed and toasted

Toasted nuts, stem ginger and raisins, enveloped in dark, bitter chocolate with a hint of brandy, and coated in white chocolate and flaked almonds…an irresistible treat. Keep in the fridge for up to a week and slice off thin rounds as required.

1 Put the plain chocolate and butter in a heatproof bowl set over a pan of simmering water and leave until melted.
2 Add the toasted chopped almonds, diced ginger, raisins and brandy to the chocolate, and stir gently to mix.
3 Spoon the chocolate mixture down the middle of a sheet of greaseproof paper. Wrap the greaseproof paper around the chocolate, shaping it into a roll, about 3cm (1¼in) wide. Fold the ends of the paper underneath. Refrigerate for 2 hours or until firm.
4 Melt the white chocolate in a heatproof bowl set over a pan of simmering water. Unwrap the chocolate roll. Using a palette knife quickly spread the white chocolate all over the surface of the log, then immediately roll in the toasted almonds to coat before the chocolate sets firmly. Chill for a further 1 hour until set. Serve cut into thin slices.

CHOCOLATE FUDGE

PREPARATION TIME: 15 minutes, plus cooling

COOKING TIME: 6–8 minutes

PER 25G (1OZ): 110 cals; 3g fat; 19g carbohydrate

MAKES 675G (1½LB)

225g (8oz) granulated sugar

400g can sweetened condensed milk

50g (2oz) unsalted butter

1 tbsp thin honey

1 tsp vanilla extract

100g (3½oz) plain, dark chocolate
   with 70% cocoa solids, grated

This creamy, rich fudge has an excellent chocolatey flavour and a subtle hint of vanilla. Use a sugar thermometer, if you have one, to ensure that the fudge reaches the right temperature and sets with a meltingly smooth texture.

1 Grease a 20cm (8in) square cake tin and line the base and 2.5cm (1in) up the sides with non-stick baking parchment.

2 Put the sugar, condensed milk, butter, honey and vanilla extract in a medium heavy-based saucepan and heat gently until the sugar dissolves. Bring to the boil, stirring, and boil for 6–8 minutes, stirring frequently to prevent sticking. The mixture is ready when it reaches the 'soft ball stage' and registers 115°C on a sugar thermometer. (If you don't have a thermometer, test for the soft ball stage by dropping a teaspoonful of the mixture into cold water, then rolling it between the fingers; it should form a soft ball.)

3 Remove the pan from the heat, add the grated chocolate and beat until the mixture is smooth and glossy.

4 Pour the fudge into the prepared tin, spreading it into the corners. Leave for 2 hours or until completely set.

5 Remove the fudge from the tin and peel away the lining paper. Cut into squares. Store in an airtight container.

VARIATIONS

CHOCOLATE NUT FUDGE: Stir in 50g (2oz) chopped walnuts at the end of step 3.

CHOCOLATE RUM AND RAISIN FUDGE: Add 25g (1oz) chopped raisins and 1 tbsp rum at the end of step 3.

CHOCOLATE EASTER EGG

PREPARATION TIME: 1 hour, plus setting
PER EGG: 1600 cals; 88g fat; 194g carbohydrate

MAKES 1

275–325g (10–11oz) good quality plain or milk
  chocolate, in pieces
Melted chocolate to assemble

Easter eggs are fun to make and not as difficult as you might imagine. You need at least one plastic Easter egg mould (available from specialist kitchen shops and cake decorating suppliers). The completed egg can be kept in the fridge for up to 24 hours.

1 Polish the inside of each half of a 15cm (6in) egg mould with cotton wool or a soft cloth. Put on a tray lined with non-stick baking parchment.

2 Melt the chocolate in a heatproof bowl over a pan of simmering water. Cool slightly. Pour the melted chocolate into each half-mould, tilting gently until evenly coated. Pour any excess chocolate back into the bowl.

3 Invert the moulds on to the baking parchment, then refrigerate until set. Apply a second coat of chocolate; refrigerate again. Repeat once more and refrigerate for 1 hour or until set – the egg will crack if removed too soon.

4 To turn out the egg halves, trim the excess chocolate from the outer edges of the moulds, then run the point of a knife around the edge to loosen. Carefully pull each mould away from the chocolate and press firmly – the egg halves should slip out easily. Cover loosely, then refrigerate.

5 Spread a little melted chocolate on the egg rims and, holding the other egg half in baking parchment, press on to the melted chocolate to complete the egg. Refrigerate to set; decorate with ribbons and sugar flowers.

SOLID CHOCOLATE EGGS

PREPARATION TIME: 1 hour, plus drying and setting
PER EGG: 210 cals; 12g fat; 22g carbohydrate

MAKES 12 SMALL EGGS

12 quail's eggs
450g (1lb) good quality plain, milk or white chocolate,
   in pieces

Children will love these attractive little Easter eggs. Wrap them in coloured foil and arrange in small baskets, or hide them for a traditional Easter egg hunt! For marbled eggs use a combination of milk or plain and white chocolate.

1 Blow the eggs: using a needle, pierce a tiny hole in each end of an egg and gently blow out the contents. Enlarge the hole in one end so it's big enough to take a small piping nozzle, then wash out the shell with cold water. Leave in a warm place to dry while you blow the remaining eggs. When all the shells are completely dry, apply sticky tape over each tiny hole so it can't leak.

2 Melt the chocolate in a heatproof bowl over a pan of gently simmering water. (If using different types of chocolate, melt them separately.) Spoon into nylon piping bag(s) fitted with a small plain nozzle and pipe into the shells through the larger holes, swirling it around from time to time to remove any air bubbles (use a mix of chocolates for a marbled effect). Leave to set overnight in the fridge.

3 Carefully crack the eggs and peel off the shells. Wrap each chocolate egg tightly in coloured foil, then put in egg cups or arrange in a basket.

VARIATION: Use ordinary hen's eggs instead of quail's eggs to make larger eggs. The above quantity of chocolate is sufficient to make 4.

RICH CHOCOLATE SAUCE

PREPARATION TIME: 5 minutes
COOKING TIME: 5 minutes
PER SERVING: 150 cals; 12g fat; 6g carbohydrate

SERVES 6

125g (4oz) plain, dark chocolate
   with 70% cocoa solids, in pieces
25g (1oz) unsalted butter
2 tbsp Grand Marnier, or other liqueur of your choice
   (optional)

This smooth, dark chocolate sauce is equally good served warm or cool, poured over ice cream, profiteroles, or traditional steamed or baked puddings.

1 Put the chocolate in a small heavy-based pan with 150ml (¼ pint) water. Stir constantly over a low heat until the chocolate is melted, then bring to the boil, stirring.
2 Let bubble for 1 minute, then remove from the heat and stir in the butter, and liqueur if using.

VARIATION: Omit the liqueur. Add 1–2 tbsp light muscovado sugar to the water with the chocolate in step 1.

CHOCOLATE FUDGE SAUCE

PREPARATION TIME: 5 minutes
COOKING TIME: 5 minutes
PER SERVING: 210 cals; 18g fat; 11g carbohydrate

SERVES 6

50g (2oz) unsalted butter
50g (2oz) light muscovado sugar
50g (2oz) plain, dark chocolate
   with at least 60% cocoa solids, in pieces
100ml (3½fl oz) double cream

A rich, creamy, chocolate sauce to serve warm poured over ice cream, poached pears, bananas or steamed puddings. Add a tablespoonful of rum, brandy or liqueur to the finished sauce if you like.

1 Put the butter, sugar and chocolate in a small heavy-based pan and heat gently until the chocolate is melted.
2 Pour in the cream, slowly bring to the boil and let bubble for 3 minutes until the sauce is glossy and thickened.
3 Allow the sauce to cool slightly before serving.

CHOCOLATE CRÈME ANGLAISE

PREPARATION TIME: 20 minutes, plus infusing

COOKING TIME: 10–20 minutes

PER SERVING: 160 cals; 10g fat; 11g carbohydrate

SERVES 4

300ml (½ pint) milk

50g (2oz) plain, dark chocolate
   with at least 60% cocoa solids, in pieces

1 vanilla pod, split

3 egg yolks, beaten

1 tbsp golden caster sugar

Silky smooth 'real' chocolate custard is a decadent treat to accompany special desserts. It can be served hot or cold.

1 Pour the milk into a heavy-based saucepan and add the chocolate and vanilla pod. Heat slowly until the chocolate has melted and the mixture is almost boiling. Take off the heat and set aside to infuse for about 20 minutes. Remove the vanilla pod.

2 Whisk the egg yolks and sugar together in a bowl until thick and creamy. Gradually whisk in the hot chocolate milk, then strain back into the pan.

3 Cook over a low heat, stirring constantly, for 10–20 minutes until the custard thickens enough to lightly coat the back of the wooden spoon; do not allow to boil or the custard may curdle.

4 Serve warm or, if serving cold, pour into a chilled bowl, cover with a disc of dampened greaseproof paper to prevent a skin forming and set aside to cool.

COOK'S TIP: It's essential to avoid overheating the custard otherwise it is liable to curdle. As a precaution, you can beat 1 tsp cornflour with the egg yolks at step 1. This helps to stabilise the custard, but must be cooked through over gentle heat otherwise it will adversely affect the flavour.

VARIATION: For an extra rich creamy custard sauce, replace half of the milk with single cream.

CHOCOLATE GANACHE

PREPARATION TIME: 10 minutes, plus cooling
PER SERVING: 280 cals; 26g fat; 8g carbohydrate

SERVES 8

225g (8oz) plain, dark chocolate
    with 60–70% cocoa solids, chopped into small pieces
250ml (8fl oz) double cream

Ganache is wonderfully versatile. Serve it warm as a rich sauce for ice cream or poached pears. At room temperature it makes a superb, smooth coating for special cakes – its characteristic use. Chill it lightly and you can use it to fill meringues, choux buns or sandwich cakes. Chilled thoroughly until firm, ganache forms the basis for classic truffles.

1 Put the chocolate in a medium heatproof bowl. Pour the cream into a small heavy-based pan and bring to the boil.
2 Immediately pour the cream on to the chocolate and stir gently in one direction until the chocolate has melted and the mixture is smooth. Set aside to cool for 5 minutes.
3 Whisk the ganache until it begins to hold its shape. Used at room temperature, the mixture should be the consistency of softened butter.

CHOCOLATE FUDGE FROSTING

PREPARATION TIME: 5 minutes
COOKING TIME: 5 minutes
PER 25G (1OZ): 135 cals; 5g fat; 25g carbohydrate

MAKES 400G (14OZ)

50g (2oz) butter
125g (4oz) light muscovado sugar
75g (3oz) plain chocolate, in pieces
2 tbsp single cream or milk
200g (7oz) icing sugar, sifted

A dark, rich frosting that can be swirled attractively over a cake, using a palette knife. This quantity is sufficient to fill and cover the top of a 20cm (8in) cake.

1 Put the butter, sugar, chocolate and cream in a saucepan. Heat gently until the sugar dissolves, then bring to the boil and boil briskly for 3 minutes.
2 Remove from the heat and gradually stir in the icing sugar. Beat with a wooden spoon for 1 minute until smooth.
3 Use immediately, spreading with a wet palette knife, or dilute with a little water to use as a smooth coating.

CHOCOLATE BUTTERCREAM

PREPARATION TIME: 5 minutes

PER 25G (1OZ): 220 cals; 11g fat; 31g carbohydrate

MAKES 250G (9OZ)

1 tbsp cocoa powder
75g (3oz) unsalted butter, softened
175g (6oz) icing sugar, sifted
Few drops of vanilla extract
1–2 tbsp milk or water

This quantity of buttercream is sufficient to fill and cover the top of an 18cm (7in) cake. To coat the sides as well, use 110g (4oz) butter and 225g (8oz) icing sugar. For a decorative effect, swirl the buttercream with a palette knife, or mark lines with the prongs of a fork.

1 Blend the cocoa powder with 2 tbsp boiling water and set aside to cool.
2 Put the butter in a bowl and beat with a wooden spoon until it is light and fluffy. Gradually stir in the icing sugar. Add the blended cocoa, vanilla extract and milk or water, and beat well until light and smooth.

VARIATION: Omit the cocoa powder and water. Instead, flavour the buttercream with 25–40g (1–1½oz) plain chocolate, melted and cooled until barely warm.

CHOCOLATE GLACÉ ICING

PREPARATION TIME: 5 minutes

PER 25G (1OZ): 180 cals; trace fat;
47g carbohydrate

MAKES 225G (8OZ)

2 tsp cocoa powder
225g (8oz) icing sugar, sifted
Few drops of vanilla extract (optional)

This amount is sufficient to cover the top of an 18cm (7in) cake or up to 18 small cakes.

1 Blend the cocoa powder with 1 tbsp hot water to a smooth paste and set aside to cool.
2 Mix the icing sugar and cocoa paste together in a bowl, adding the vanilla extract if wished. Using a wooden spoon, gradually stir in 2–3 tbsp hot water until the mixture is the consistency of thick cream. Beat until the icing is smooth and thick enough to coat the back of the spoon.

INDEX

Page numbers in *italic* refer to photographs

B

Baked Alaskas, double chocolate 29, 29
Bananas:
    Banana and chocolate bread pudding 22
    Chocolate and banana crêpes 34
    Chocolate and banana roll 114, 115
    Chocolate banana muffins 90, 91
Bread pudding, banana and chocolate 22
Brownies:
    cherry chocolate fudge 88, 89
    gluten-free 86
    pecan fudge 107
    the ultimate chocolate 86, 87
    white chocolate and macadamia nut 106
Buttercream, chocolate 141

C

Cakes:
    The best chocolate cake in the world 128,
      129
    Chocolate and Grand Marnier cake 120, 121
    Chocolate cake with cherry topping 122, 123
    Chocolate ribbon cake 124, 125
    Cosmic chocolate cake 110, 110
    Egg-free chocolate layer cake 83
    Farmhouse chocolate cake 84
    Gluten-free chocolate cake 82, 82
    Simple chocolate cake 84
    Two-tone chocolate cake 118, 119
    Ultra-dark chocolate cake with raspberries
      126, 127
    see also Devil's food cake; Marble cake; Tiffin
      cake
Cheesecake, orange and chocolate 49
Cherries:
    Cherry chip cookies 101, 101
    Cherry chocolate fudge brownies 88, 89
    Chocolate and cherry amaretti tart 32, 33
    Chocolate cake with cherry topping 122, 123
    Mini chocolate and cherry puddings 18, 19
Chocolate:
    melting 9, 9
    quality 8
    storing 9
    types of 8–9
Chocolate pots, rich 38, 39

Choux buns, chocolate 104, 105
Choux paste 59
Cocoa beans, quality of 8
Cocoa solids 8
Cookies:
    Cherry chip cookies 101, 101
    Chocolate chip cookies 99
    White and dark chocolate cookies 100
Couverture 8
Crackles, chocolate 92
Cream, vanilla 27, 46
Crème anglaise, chocolate 139
Crêpes:
    Chocolate and banana crêpes 34
    Chocolate crêpes with a boozy sauce 34, 35
Croquembouche, chocolate 59
Crumb pudding, chocolate 17
Cup cakes, vanilla and white chocolate 76, 77
Curls, traditional 10, 10
Custard 124
    Baked chocolate and coffee custards 41
Cut-outs, chocolate 11, 11

D

Devil's food cake 85

E

Easter egg, chocolate 136, 136
Egg-free chocolate layer cake 83
Eggs, solid chocolate 137
Energy bars, fruity 96

F

Florentines 98
Frosting, chocolate fudge 140
Fruit:
    Chocolate dipped fruit 13, 13
    Chocolate dipped fruit and nuts 134
    Figgy fruit slices 96
    Fruity energy bars 96
    White chocolate and red fruit trifle 42, 43
Fudge, chocolate 135

G

Ganache toppings/fillings, chocolate 54, 80,
    108, 119, 122, 128, 140
    white 118, 119
Gâteau, hazelnut meringue 62

Glacé icing, chocolate 141
Gluten-free:
    brownies 86
    chocolate cake 82, 82

I

Ice cream:
    chocolate 70
    mocha 72
    tiramisu 72, 73

L

Leaves, chocolate 13, 13
Liqueurs and spirits:
    Brandy truffles 132, 133
    Chocolate and Grand Marnier cake 120, 121
    Chocolate brandy torte 112, 113
    Grand Marnier truffles 132, 133

M

Macaroon, chestnut and chocolate 60, 61
Marble cake, chocolate 80, 81
Meringue 62, 63, 64, 65
    Chocolate and hazelnut meringues 64
Mousse, chocolate 38, 54, 120
    Layered chocolate mousse cake terrine 48
    Rich chocolate mousse cake 111
Muffins, chocolate banana 90, 91

N

Nuts:
    Almond and white chocolate tart 53
    Chestnut and chocolate macaroon 60, 61
    Chocolate and hazelnut meringues 64
    Chocolate and hazelnut tart 54, 55
    Chocolate dipped fruit and nuts 134
    Chocolate nut slice 134
    Hazelnut meringue gâteau 62
    Hazelnut paste 54
    Pecan fudge brownies 107
    White chocolate and macadamia nut
        brownies 106

O

Orange:
    Chocolate, prune and orange soufflés 26, 26
    Chocolate and orange truffle torte 56, 57
    Orange and chocolate cheesecake 49

P

Pain au chocolat 30
Panettone pudding, chocolate 23
Panna cotta, boozy 40, 40
Pavlova, strawberry and chocolate 63
Pears:
    Pear galettes with chocolate sauce 30, 31
    Spicy poached pears with chocolate sauce 68, 69
Piped decorations 12, 12, 110, 110
Profiteroles 58
Prunes:
    Chocolate, prune and orange soufflés 26, 26
    Chocolate and prune roulade 67
Puddings:
    Dark puddings with white chocolate custard 20, 20
    Mmini chocolate and cherry puddings 18, 19
    Quick gooey chocolate puddings 16, 16
    see also Crumb pudding; Sponge pudding

R

Raspberries:
    Raspberries with chocolate mallow 28, 28
    Raspberry and white chocolate tarts 51
    Ultra-dark chocolate cake with raspberries 126, 127
Ribbons, chocolate 11, 11, 124, 125
Roll, chocolate and banana 114, 115
Roulade:
    Black Forest roulade 66, 66
    Chocolate and prune roulade 67
    Chocolate meringue roulade 65, 65
    Chocolate roulade 116, 117

S

Sachertorte 108, 109
Sauces:
    chocolate 58, 68
    chocolate fudge 59, 138
    rich chocolate 138
    vanilla 46
    white chocolate 107
Shortbread, chocolate fudge 97, 97
Slices:
    Chocolate nut slice 134
    Figgy fruit slices 96
    Wicked chocolate slices 94, 95

ACKNOWLEDGEMENTS

Sorbet, chocolate cinnamon 70, 71
Soufflés:
    Chocolate, prune and orange soufflés 26, 26
    Chocolate soufflés with vanilla cream 27
    Cold chocolate soufflé 45
    Gooey chocolate soufflés 24, 25
    Mocha soufflés 24
Sponge pudding, chocolate steamed 17
Strawberries:
    Strawberry and chocolate Pavlova 63
    Strawberry chocolate tart 52
Swiss roll, chocolate 79

T

Tarts:
    Almond and white chocolate tart 53
    Chocolate and cherry amaretti tart 32, 32
    Chocolate and hazelnut tart 54, 55
    Raspberry and white chocolate tarts 51
    Strawberry chocolate tart 52
Terrine, rich chocolate, with vanilla sauce 46, 47
Tiffin cake 92, 93
Tiramisu:
    Ice cream tiramisu 72, 73
    Vanilla tiramisu 44, 44
Torte:
    Baked ricotta torte 50, 50
    Chocolate and orange truffle torte 56, 57
    Chocolate brandy torte 112, 113
    see also Sachertorte
Trifle, white chocolate and red fruit 42, 43
Truffle mixture 56
Truffles:
    Brandy truffles 132, 133
    Grand Marnier truffles 132, 133

V

Valrhona chocolate 8
Victoria sandwich, chocolate 78
Viennese fingers, chocolate 98

Techniques photography on pages 9-13 by Craig Robertson.

Other photography: pages 2, 35, 39, 44, 73 Marie-Louise Avery; pages 19, 71, 109 Steve Baxter; pages 57, 81, 123 Jean Cazals; pages 26, 29, 50, 65, 69, 82, 125 Laurie Evans; pages 61, 117 Graham Kirk; pages 93, 133 Sandra Lane; pages 16, 25, 87 William Lingwood; page 110 James Merrell; pages 90, 113, 114 David Munns; pages 118, 121, 127 James Murphy; page 77 Michael Paul; pages 55 George Seper; pages 89, 101 Roger Stowell; pages 5, 97, 105 Clive Streeter; pages 95, 129 Martin Thompson; pages 21, 28, 31, 40, 66 Plilip Webb; pages 43, 47 Tim Winter; page 33 Elizabeth Zeschin.